Study Guide to Accompany

STATISTICS FOR THE BEHAVIORAL SCIENCES

SECOND EDITION

A First Course for Students of Psychology and Education

Frederick J Gravetter
Department of Psychology
State University of New York
College at Brockport

Larry B. Wallnau
Department of Psychology
State University of New York
College at Brockport

Prepared by
Frederick J Gravetter

West Publishing Company
St. Paul   New York   Los Angeles   San Francisco

••• CONTENTS •••

··· PREFACE ···

There is a very old joke about a lost and confused tourist who asks a New Yorker for directions: "How do you get to Carnegie Hall?" And the reply is, "Practice, kid, practice." This punch line could easily be the motto for a statistics course. We encourage students to work as many exercises as they can because, like any other skill, understanding and using statistics requires practice. Lots of practice.

This Study Guide gives you a chance to review what you have studied in the text and it provides additional exercises for you to practice. We must emphasize that you should work in the Study Guide only <u>after</u> you have read and studied the corresponding chapter in the book. The Study Guide is a supplement to the text, it by no means can replace it. Every chapter in the text has a corresponding Study Guide chapter, and each Study Guide chapter has six major sections. These sections are described here.

<u>Learning Objectives</u>. The Study Guide chapters begin with a list of goals that should be achieved upon completion of studying a text chapter. These objectives usually are task-oriented, pointing to specific things you should know how to do or how to explain. If you lack confidence in meeting any of these objectives, you should return to the appropriate section(s) of the text for further study.

<u>New Terms And Concepts</u>. This section consists of a list of important terms and concepts that appeared in the text. You should identify or define these terms, and explain how closely-related terms are interrelated. Return to the text to check your answers.

<u>New Formulas</u>.   A list of formulas that were introduced in the text is provided. For each formula, you should test yourself in the following way:
  1) Identify each symbol and term in the formula.
  2) Make a list of the computational steps that are indicated by the formula.
  3) Describe when each formula is used and explain why it is used or what it is computing.

<u>Step-By-Step</u>.   This section presents a typical problem (or problems) from the chapter and provides a demonstration of the step-by-step procedures for solving the problem.

<u>Hints and Cautions</u>.   In this section, we provide advice on the typical mistakes students make, and the difficulties they commonly have with the chapter material.

<u>Self-Test and Review</u>.   In this section we present a series of questions and problems that provide a general review of the

chapter. As much as possible, the problems consist of simple
sets of numbers so that you can solve them with minimal
calculation. Work through this Self-Test carefully, and
remember that your mistakes will tell you what areas need
additional study. Incidentally, the Answers to the Self-Test
are given at the end of each Study Guide chapter. For
problems with numerical answers, do not fret about slight
differences between your answer and ours. A little rounding
error is to be expected.

STUDY HINTS

It seems appropriate for a study guide to have a few
suggestions to help you study. The following are some hints
that have proved useful for our own students.

1.   You will learn (and remember) much more if you study
for short periods several times a week, rather than try
to condense all your studying into one long session. For
example, it is far more effective to study for one-half
hour every night than to spend a single 3 and one-half
hour session once a week.

2.   Do some work before class. Read the appropriate
sections in the textbook before your instructor presents
the material in class. Although you may not completely
understand what you read, you will have a general idea of
the topic which will make the lecture easier to follow.
Also, you can identify items that are particularly
confusing and then be sure that these items are clarified
in class.

3.   Pay attention and think during class. Although this
may sound like obvious advice, many students spend their
class time frantically taking notes rather than listening
and understanding what is being said. For example, it
usually is not necessary to copy down every sample
problem that your instructor works in class. There are
plenty of example problems in your textbook and in this
study guide - you probably do not need one more in your
notebook. Just put down your pencil and pay attention.
Be sure that you understand what is being done, and try
to anticipate the next step in the problem.

4.   Test yourself regularly. Do not wait until the end
of the chapter or the end of the week to check your
knowledge. After each lecture, work some of the end-of-
chapter problems, do the learning checks, and be sure you
can define key terms. If you are having trouble, get
your questions answered immediately (re-read the text, go
to your instructor, ask questions in class). Do not let
yourself fall behind.

5.   Don't kid yourself. Many students sit in class
watching the instructor solve problems, and think to
themselves, "This looks easy, I understand it." Do you
really? Can you do the problem all by yourself?

      Many students use the examples in the textbook
as a guide for working assigned problems. They begin the
problem, get stuck, then check the example to see what to
do next. A minute later they are stuck again, so they
take another peek at the example in the text.
Eventually, the problem is finished and the students
think that they understand how to solve problems.
Although there is nothing wrong with using examples as

models for solving problems, you should try working a problem with your book closed to determine whether you can complete it on your own.

Finally a few tips to help you prepare for exams.

1.   Perhaps the best way to get ready for an exam is to make up your own exams. This is particularly effective if you have a friend in the class so you can both make up exams and then exchange them. Constructing your own exam forces you to identify the important points in the material, and it makes you think about how exam questions might be phrased. It is very satisfying to open a statistics exam and find some questions that you wrote yourself the day before.

2.   Many students suffer from "exam anxiety" which causes them to freeze up and forget everything during exams. One way to help avoid the problem is for you to take charge of your own time during an exam.
     a.   Don't spend a lot of time working on one problem that you really don't understand (especially if it is a 1-point true/false question). Just move on to the rest of the exam - you can come back later, if you have time.
     b.   Remember that you do not have to finish the exam questions in the order they are presented. When you get your exam, go immediately to the problems you understand best.   This will build some confidence and make you better prepared for the remainder of the exam.

Probably the best way to reduce exam anxiety is to practice taking exams. Make up your own exam (select problems from the book and study guide) or have a friend make up an exam. Then

try to duplicate the general conditions of an exam. Put your
book away if you are not allowed to use it during exams. Give
yourself a time limit. If you have an old alarm clock, set it
in front of you so that you can hear the ticking and watch the
time slip away. You might even try sitting in front of a
mirror so that every time you look up there is someone
watching you.

Finally, remember that very few miracles happen during exams.
The work on your exam is usually a good reflection of your
studying and understanding. Most students walk into an exam
with a very good idea of how well they will do. Be honest
with yourself. If you are well prepared, you will do well on
the exam, and there is no reason to panic. If you are not
prepared then you are in trouble and you cannot blame "exam
anxiety" for your problems.

CHAPTER 1 INTRODUCTION TO STATISTICS

LEARNING OBJECTIVES

1. You should be familiar with the terminology and special notation of statistical methods.

2. You should understand the purpose of statistics: When, how, and why they are used.

3. You should understand summation notation and be able to use this notation to represent mathematical operations and to compute specified sums.

NEW TERMS AND CONCEPTS

The following terms were introduced in this chapter. Define or describe each term and, where appropriate, describe how each term is related to other terms in the list.

population — *whole group*
sample — *part of a group*
statistic — *describes characteristics of a sample*
parameter — *" " population*

descriptive statistics

inferential statistics

variable

constant

raw score

dependent variable

independent variable

correlational method

experimental method

control group

experimental group

confounding variable

hypothesis

hypothetical construct

operational definition

nominal scale

ordinal scale

interval scale

ratio scale

discrete variable

continuous variable

Σ (sigma)

N

X

STEP-BY-STEP

Summation Notation: In statistical calculations you constantly will be required to add a set of values to find a specific total. We will use algebraic expressions to represent the values being added (for example, X = score), and we will use the Greek letter sigma (Σ) to signify the process of summation. Occasionally, you simply will be adding a set of scores, ΣX. More often, you will be doing some initial computation and then adding the results. For example, we will

routinely need to square each score and then find the sum of
the squared values, ΣX^2. The following step-by-step process
should help you understand summation notation and use it
correctly to find appropriate totals.

Step 1: The first step in using summation correctly is
to identify the "term" or "algebraic expression" that
follows the summation sign. There are 3 general rules to
help you identify the "term."
   a. Everything within parenthesis is part of the same
       term.
   b. If several things are being multiplied together,
       they are all part of the same term.
   c. If something is squared, the squared sign is part
       of the term.

Cover the answers in the right-hand column, and
identify the term being summed for each of the following
expressions.

$\Sigma X + 3$	X
$\Sigma (X + 3)$	$X + 3$
$\Sigma X^2 - 2$	X^2
$\Sigma (X - 5)^2$	$(X - 5)^2$
ΣX^2	X^2
$\Sigma XY + 5$	XY

Step 2: The original X values should be listed in a
column. Use the "term" you identified from Step 1 as a
new column heading, and list all of the appropriate
values for this term under the new heading.
   Suppose your task is to find $\Sigma (X + 3)$. The "term"
in this expression is $(X + 3)$, so use this as a column

heading and list all of the (X + 3) values next to the
original X values.

X	(X + 3)
4	7
8	11
2	5
6	9

Note: Occasionally you will need more than one column to get
to the final term you want.   To compute $\Sigma(X + 3)^2$, for
example, begin with the X column, then add a column of (X + 3)
values, and then add a third column that squares each of the
(X + 3) values.

X	(X + 3)	$(X + 3)^2$
4	7	49
8	11	121
2	5	25
6	9	81

Step 3:   Simply add all the values in the column headed
by the term identified in Step 1.

Using the same numbers that we used in Step 2, you
find $\Sigma(X + 3)$ by simply adding the values in the (X + 3)
column.

$$\Sigma(X + 3) = 7 + 11 + 5 + 9 = 32$$

To find $\Sigma(X + 3)^2$ you add the values in the $(X + 3)^2$
column.

$$\Sigma(X + 3)^2 = 49 + 121 + 25 + 81 = 276$$

1. Many students confuse the independent variable and the dependent variable in an experiment. It may help you to differentiate these terms if you visualize an experiment as a big black box filled with people.

Independent Variable: The scientist (in a white lab-coat) stands outside the box and <u>independently</u> manipulates things (visualize knobs on the box that control things like temperature, background noise, etc.). The variable manipulated or controlled by the scientist is the independent variable.

Dependent Variable: Meanwhile, the purpose of the experiment is to see whether the people inside the box will respond to the scientist's manipulations. In other words, will the people's responses <u>depend</u> on what the scientist is doing. The dependent variable is the set of responses that the scientist observes and measures.

2. Many students look at summation notation as if it were only a verb or a command. For example, the expression ΣX is seen as an instruction to add a set of scores. However, you also should realize that the expression ΣX is a thing or a noun. Specifically, ΣX is the "total" for a set of scores. In later chapters you will encounter summation notation in more complex formulas. Often it will be useful to see a summation expression as a "thing" that you can manipulate, rather than as a command that you simply follow.

3. There are three specific sums that are used repeatedly in statistics calculations. You should be familiar with the notation and computations for each of the following:

a. ΣX^2 First square each score, then add the
                          squared values.

b. $(\Sigma X)^2$ First sum the scores, then square the
                          total.

c. $\Sigma(X - C)^2$ First subtract the constant C from each
                          score, then square each of the resulting
                          values. Finally, add the squared
                          numbers.

SELF-TEST AND REVIEW

1. The field of statistics encompasses various methods
and procedures for organizing and interpreting data.
Statistical techniques are classified into two major
categories: _Descriptive_ and _Inferential_. Describe the
general purpose for each of these categories.

2.   A researcher generally begins with a question
concerning a group of individuals called a population.
However, populations are usually too large to study in
the laboratory, so most research is done with samples.
Define _population_ and _sample_.

3.   In very broad terms, the goal of scientific
investigation is to find relationships between variables.
The process of gathering data to examine relationships
can be accomplished by either the _correlational method_ or
the _experimental method_.
    a. Describe these two methods.
    b. Identify the strengths and weakness of each
method.

c.   A researcher wants to examine the relationship between family size and political attitude for a group of 100 college students. Each student is asked to report the number of individuals in his/her immediate family and each student completes an attitude questionnaire that measures political opinions. Does this study use the correlational method or the experimental method?

4.   In the experimental method, the scientist is examining the relationship between an independent variable and a dependent variable.
   a.   In general terms, define the independent and dependent variables.
   b.   A recent study reports that infant rats fed a special protein-enriched diet reached an adult weight 10% greater than littermates raised on a regular diet. For this study, what is the independent variable? What is the dependent variable?

5.   The data that a scientist collects usually consist of measurements. The process of measuring requires that individuals be classified into different categories, and the set of categories makes up a scale of measurement. We identified four types of measurement scales: <u>Nominal</u>, <u>Ordinal</u>, <u>Interval</u>, and <u>Ratio</u>. Briefly describe each.

6.   One of the primary goals of descriptive statistics is to summarize a large set of data with a simple descriptive characteristic. A good example is the common practice of summarizing a large group of scores by reporting the average value. The descriptive characteristics that summarize a large group of scores are called either <u>statistics</u> or <u>parameters</u>. Define statistic and parameter.

7.   The Greek letter sigma, represented by the symbol Σ,
is used to stand for "the sum of." This summation
notation is used in equations to represent specific sums
and it is used to describe specific mathematical
operations. For example, "the sum of the scores" would
be written ΣX. The process of adding three points to
each individual score and then computing the total of the
resulting values would be written $\Sigma(X + 3)$.

   a.   Compute each value requested for the following
set of scores.

	$\underline{X}$
ΣX	1
ΣX^2	3
$(\Sigma X)^2$	5
N	2

   b.   Compute each value requested for the following
set of scores.

	$\underline{X}$
$\Sigma X + 1$	0
$\Sigma(X + 1)$	6
$\Sigma(X + 1)^2$	2
	3

8.   Although you should be able to read summation
notation and perform the appropriate operations, you also
should be able to write summation notation to express
specific operations. Use summation notation to express
each of the following calculations.

   a.   Add 3 points to each score, then find the sum of
the resulting values.

   b.   Find the sum of the scores, then add 10 points
to the total.

c.   Subtract 1 point from each score, then square
each of the resulting values. Next, find the sum of the
squared numbers. Finally, add 5 points to this sum.

ANSWERS TO SELF-TEST

1.   The general purpose of descriptive statistics is to
simplify the organization and presentation of data. The
purpose of inferential statistics is to use the data from
a sample to draw general conclusions about a population.

2.   A population is the entire group of individuals that
a researcher would like to study. A sample is a part of
the population. Usually, experiments are done with
samples, but researchers would like to generalize the
results to the entire population.

3.   a.   In the correlational method the researcher simply
observes and measures two variables. No attempt is made
to control or manipulate either variable. In the
experimental method the researcher manipulates one
variable and then observes whether the manipulation has
any effect on a second variable.
      b.   The strength of the correlational method is that
it is completely natural. The researcher is not creating
an artificial situation or influencing the results.
However, it is difficult to establish a cause-effect
relation between two variables with the correlational
method because the researcher cannot control confounding
variables. The strength of the experimental method is
control. The researcher can manipulate one variable
while holding all others constant. In this way, it is
possible to establish a direct cause-effect relation

between two variables. The weakness of the experimental
method is that researchers often must create artificial
environments in order to maintain control.

    c. This study uses the correlational method. the
researcher is simply observing variables, not controlling/
manipulating them.

4. a. The variable that is manipulated by the
researcher is the independent variable. The variable
that is observed and measured is the dependent variable.
    b. The independent variable is the type of diet and
the dependent variable is the weight of the rats.

5. A nominal scale consists of categories that are
differentiated by names. In an ordinal scale, the
categories are rank ordered. In an interval scale, the
categories are all the same size or magnitude, and they
are ordered. A ratio scale is an interval scale that has
a real zero point.

6. A statistic is a descriptive characteristic of a
sample. A parameter is a descriptive characteristic of a
population.

7. a. $\Sigma X = 11$, $\Sigma X^2 = 39$, $(\Sigma X)^2 = 121$, $N = 4$

    b. $\Sigma X + 1 = 12$, $\Sigma(X + 1) = 15$, $\Sigma(X + 1)^2 = 75$

8. a. $\Sigma(X + 3)$

    b. $\Sigma X + 10$

    c. $\Sigma(X - 1)^2 + 5$

CHAPTER **2** FREQUENCY DISTRIBUTIONS

LEARNING OBJECTIVES

1. Know how to organize data into regular or grouped frequency distribution tables.

2. Be able to construct graphs, including bar graphs, histograms, and polygons.

3. Be able to describe the shape of a distribution portrayed in a frequency distribution graph.

4. Know how to construct stem and leaf displays.

5. Be able to determine percentiles and percentile ranks, using interpolation when necessary.

NEW TERMS AND CONCEPTS

The following terms were introduced in this chapter.
Define or describe each term and, where appropriate, describe
how each term is related to other terms in the list.

        frequency distribution
        grouped frequency distribution
        range
        class interval
        upper real limit
        lower real limit
        apparent limits
        histogram
        bar graph
        polygon
        symmetrical distribution
        positively skewed distribution
        negatively skewed distribution
        tail(s) of a distribution
        percentile
        percentile rank
        cumulative frequency (cf)
        cumulative percentage (c%)
        interpolation
      stem and leaf display

NEW FORMULAS

$$\text{proportion} = p = \frac{f}{N}$$

$$\text{percentage} = p(100) = \frac{f}{N}(100)$$

range = high - low + 1

$$c\% = \frac{cf}{N}(100)$$

STEP-BY-STEP

Interpolation: Because it is impossible to report an infinite number of possible data points, nearly all tables and graphs show only a limited number of selected values. However, researchers often want to examine data points that fall between the reported values. The process of interpolation provides a method for estimating intermediate values.

In this chapter we used interpolation to find percentiles and percentile ranks that cannot be read directly from a frequency distribution table. The following example will be used to demonstrate this process.

The problem is to find the 70th percentile for the distribution shown in the table. Because 70% is not one of the cumulative percentages listed in the table (it is between 65% and 90%), we must use interpolation.

X	f	cf	c%
25-29	1	20	100%
20-24	1	19	95%
15-19	5	18	90%
10-14	9	13	65%
5-9	4	4	20%

Step 1: Identify the interval that contains the intermediate value you want.

In this example we are looking for the score that has a rank of 70%. The intermediate value, 70%, is located between the reported values of 65% and 90%.

Step 2: Draw a sketch showing the interval you identified in Step 1. Show the two end points of the interval and identify the location of the intermediate value within this interval.
For this example,

```
                          c%
                          90%


                                   ---70%
                          65%
```

Step 3: Expand your sketch by placing the second scale beside the one you have drawn. Then find the end-points of the interval on the second scale. Remember, each cumulative percentage value is associated with the upper real limit of the score interval.

```
                    X        c%
                  19.5      90%


        ? ----                    ---- 70%
                  14.5      65%
```

Step 4: Look at your sketch and make a common-sense estimate of the final answer. In this example, the value we want is located between 14.5 and 19.5. It appears to be closer to the 14.5 end of the interval, probably around X = 15. (If you make this kind of preliminary estimate, it can save you from making a careless mistake later.)

Step 5: Find the precise location of the intermediate value within the interval. This step requires that you compute a fraction,

$$fraction = \frac{distance\ from\ top\ of\ interval}{interval\ width}$$

For this example, the intermediate value of 70% is located 20 points from the top of the interval, and the total interval is 25 points (from 90% to 65%). Thus, our fraction is,

fraction = 20/25 = 4/5 = .80

In this case, the intermediate position we want is located 4/5ths of the way down from the top of the interval.

Step 6: Take the fraction from Step 5, and apply it to the other scale. In this example, we want to find the position that is 4/5ths of the way down from the top on the score side of the scale.

The total distance on the score side is 5 points (from 19.5 to 14.5). To find 4/5ths of this distance, you simply multiply:

(4/5)(5 points) = 4 points

Thus, the position we want is located 4 points down from the top of score interval.

Step 7: Compute the final value by starting at the top of the interval and counting down the distance you computed in Step 6. In this example, the top of the score interval is 19.5 and we want to count down 4 points. The final answer is,

19.5 - 4 = 15.5

We have determined that a percentile rank of 70% corresponds
to a score of X = 15.5. (Note that this answer is in
agreement with the preliminary estimate that we made in Step
4. If there is a contradiction at this point, you should
check your calculations.)

HINTS AND CAUTIONS

1.   When making the list of intervals for a grouped
frequency distribution table, some people find it easier
to begin the list with the lowest interval and work up to
the highest. Fewer mistakes will be made.

2.   When using interpolation, it is very helpful to
sketch a table that shows the range of values on each
scale.

3.   When determining a percentile rank, remember that
the cumulative frequencies in a grouped frequency
distribution table correspond to the upper real limits of
their class intervals.

SELF-TEST AND REVIEW

1.   Simplifying and organizing data is the goal of
descriptive statistics. One descriptive technique is to
organize a set of scores in a frequency distribution.
Define a frequency distribution and explain how it
simplifies and organizes data.

2. A frequency distribution can be presented either as a graph or a table.

   a. Describe the basic elements in a frequency distribution table.

   b. Describe the basic elements of a frequency distribution graph.

3. Occasionally it is necessary to group scores into class intervals and construct a grouped frequency distribution.

   a. Explain when it is necessary to use a grouped table (as opposed to a regular table).

   b. Outline the guidelines for constructing a grouped frequency table.

4. A frequency distribution graph can be either a histogram, a bargraph, or a polygon. Define each of these graphs and identify the circumstances where each is used.

5. For a continuous variable each score actually corresponds to an interval on the scale of measurement.

   a. In general terms define the real limits of an interval.

   b. If a distribution has scores of 10, 9, 8, etc., what are the real limits for X = 8?

   c. If a distribution has scores of 5.5, 5.0, 4.5, 4.0, etc., what are the real limits for X = 4.5?

   d. In a grouped frequency distribution, each class interval has real limits and apparent limits. What are the real and apparent limits for the interval 10-14?

6. For the following set of scores:

8, 7, 10, 12, 9, 11, 10, 9, 12, 11

7, 9, 7, 10, 10, 8, 12, 7, 10, 7

a. Construct a frequency distribution table including columns for frequency, proportion, and percentage.

b. Draw a histogram showing these data.

c. Draw a polygon showing the data.

7. Using an interval width of 5 points, construct a grouped frequency distribution table for the following set of exam scores:

20, 31, 32, 41, 28, 52, 36, 38, 33

24, 15, 47, 58, 32, 12, 21, 34, 36

45, 27, 17, 23, 53, 36, 43

8. Beyond knowing how to construct a frequency distribution, you also should know how to read a frequency distribution. A set of data has been summarized in the following frequency distribution. Find each of the requested values for this set of data.

	X	f
a. How many scores are in the original set of data? $n = \underline{\quad}$	5	1
	4	2
b. What is the sum of	3	2
the scores (ΣX) for	2	4
the complete data set?	1	3

9. Shape is one of the basic characteristics used to describe a distribution of scores. Most distributions can be classified as being either symmetrical, positively skewed, or negatively skewed. Define each of these three shapes.

10.   Percentiles and percentile ranks are used to describe the position of individual scores within a distribution.

   a.   What does it mean to say your score is equal to the 75th percentile?

   b.   What does it mean to say that your score has a percentile rank of 40%.

******************************	X	f	cf	c%
This frequency distribution	5	4	20	100%
table will be used for	4	2	16	80%
questions 11, 12, and 13.	3	10	14	70%
******************************	2	2	4	20%
	1	2	2	10%

11.   When determining percentiles or percentile ranks, you first must find cumulative frequencies and cumulative percentages for a distribution. In a frequency distribution table each cumulative percentage value is always associated with the upper real limit of the corresponding score or interval. In the preceding table, for example, explain why c% = 80% corresponds to X = 4.5.

12.   It is possible to read some percentiles and percentile ranks directly from a table provided that the required scores are upper real limits and the required cumulative percentages are reported in the table. Using the preceding table, find each of the values requested below.

   a.   What is the 20th percentile?

   b.   What is the percentile rank for X = 3.5?

13. When a desired percentile or percentile rank is located between two known values, it is possible to estimate the desired value using the process of interpolation. Use interpolation to find each of the following values for the data in the preceding table.
   a. What is the percentile rank for X = 4.0?
   b. What is the 50th percentile?
   c. What is the 90th percentile?

14. Using the grouped table you constructed in question 7,
   a. Find the 50th percentile for this distribution.
   b. What score is needed to be in the top 40% of the distribution?
   c. What is the percentile rank for X = 42?

15. A stem and leaf display is an alternative procedure for organizing a frequency distribution. Each score is separated into a stem (the first digit or digits) and a leaf (the last digit or digits). The display consists of the stems listed in a column, with the leaf for each score written beside its stem. Construct a stem and leaf display for the data given in problem 7.

ANSWERS TO SELF-TEST

1. A frequency distribution shows the number of individuals located in each category on the scale of measurement.

2. a. In a frequency distribution table, the first column lists scores (or class intervals), and the second column lists frequencies showing the number of individuals with each score (or in each interval).

b.   In a frequency distribution graph the scores are listed on the X-axis and the frequencies are listed on the Y-axis. Usually the axes cross at the zero-point for both X and Y.

3.   a.   A grouped distribution should be used whenever the range of scores is too wide to list all the individual values in a regular table. Usually, you should use a grouped distribution if the range exceeds 15 points.

b.   To construct a grouped distribution you must select an interval width that allows the range to be completely covered with about 10 equal-sized intervals. The interval width should be an easy number (for example, 2, 5, or 10), and the bottom score in each interval should be a multiple of the width.

4.   In a histogram there is a bar above each score (or interval) showing the frequency. Adjacent bars are touching. A histogram is used with interval or ratio data. A bargraph is similar to a histogram except that there are spaces between the bars and the bargraph is used with nominal or ordinal data. In a polygon, the frequency is indicated by a dot above each score (or interval), and the dots are connected with straight lines. A polygon is used with interval or ratio data.

5. a.   The real limits for a score are the boundaries located halfway between the score and the next higher (or lower) score.
   b.   The real limits for X = 8 would be 7.5 and 8.5.
   c.   For X = 4.5, the real limits would be 4.25 and 4.75.

    d. For the class interval 10-14, the real limits are
9.5 and 14.5. The apparent limits are 10 and 14.

6. a.

X	f	p	%
12	3	.15	15%
11	2	.10	10%
10	5	.25	25%
9	3	.15	15%
8	2	.10	10%
7	5	.25	25%

b.

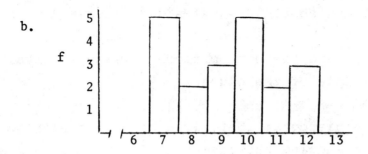

c.

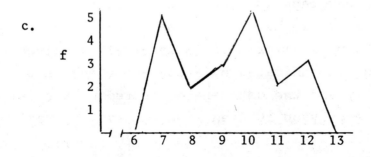

7.

X	f
55-59	1
50-54	2
45-49	2
40-44	2
35-39	4
30-34	5
25-29	2
20-24	4
15-19	2
10-14	1

8. a. n = 12   (add the frequencies)

    b. ΣX = 30   (list all 12 scores and add them)

9.   In a symmetrical distribution, the right side of the graph is a mirror image of the left side. In a positively skewed distribution, the scores pile up on the left side and taper off to the right. For a negatively skewed distribution, the scores pile up on the right and taper off to the left.

10. a. If your score is the 75th percentile, then 75% of the other individuals in the distribution have scores that are less than or equal to yours.

    b. If your score has a percentile rank of 40%, then 40% of the other individuals in the distribution have scores that are less than or equal to yours.

11.   The table indicates that 16 individuals (or 80% of the distribution) have scores of 4 or less. However, the 2 individuals with scores of X = 4 are actually located in an interval between 3.5 and 4.5. To be certain that you are including both of these individuals, you must say that 80% of the individuals in the distribution have scores less than 4.5. The cumulative percentage of 80% is associated with the upper real limit of 4.5.

12. a.   The 20th percentile is the upper real limit X = 2.5.

   b.   The upper real limit X = 3.5 has a percentile rank of 70%.

13.   a.   The score of 4.0 is located exactly in the middle of the interval from 3.5 to 4.5. The corresponding interval of percentages extends from 70% to 80%, and the exact middle of this interval is 75%. Thus, X = 4.0 has a rank of 75%.

   b.   The value 50% is located in an interval between 70% and 20%. The corresponding interval of scores extends from 3.5 to 2.5. Using interpolation, the 50th percentile is X = 3.1.

   c.   The value 90% is in an interval between 80% and 100%. The corresponding interval of scores extends from 4.5 to 5.5. Because 90% is exactly in the middle of the percentage interval, the corresponding score would be X = 5.0 which is exactly in the middle of the score interval. Thus, the 90th percentile is X = 5.0.

14. a. The 50th percentile is X = 33

    b. The boundary for the top 40% is the 60th
percentile which is X = 35.75.

    c. X = 42 has a percentile rank of 76%.

15.   1 572
       2 047831
       3 612246683
       4 5713
       5 823

CHAPTER **3** CENTRAL TENDENCY

LEARNING OBJECTIVES

1.   You should be able to define central tendency and
you should understand the general purpose of obtaining a
measure of central tendency.

2.   You should be able to define and compute each of the
three basic measures of central tendency for a set of
data.

3.   You should know when each of the three is used and
you should understand the advantages and disadvantages of
each.

4.   You should know the factors that influence central
tendency and how each factor affects each of the three
measures.

NEW TERMS AND CONCEPTS

The following terms were introduced in this chapter. Define or describe each term and, where appropriate, describe how each term is related to other terms in the list.

central tendency
mean
mode (major mode and minor mode)
weighted mean

NEW FORMULAS

$$\mu = \frac{\Sigma X}{N}$$

$$\bar{X} = \frac{\Sigma X}{n}$$

STEP-BY-STEP

The Weighted Mean: Occasionally a researcher will find it necessary to combine two (or more) sets of data, or to add new scores to an existing set of data. Rather than starting from scratch to compute the mean for the new set of data, it is possible to compute the weighted mean. To find the new mean you need two pieces of information:

1) How many scores are in the new data set?
2) What is the sum of all the scores?

Remember, the mean is the sum of the scores divided by the number. We will use the following problem to demonstrate the calculation of the weighted mean.

A researcher wants to combine the following three samples into a single group. Notice that sample 3 is actually a single score, $X = 4$. What is the mean for the combined group?

Sample 1	Sample 2	Sample 3
$n = 8$	$n = 5$	$n = 1$
$\overline{X} = 12$	$\overline{X} = 9$	$X = 4$

Step 1:   The first step is to determine n and ΣX for a
single set of data. We assume that you begin by knowing the
mean ($\overline{X}$) and number of scores (n) for the data set. With this
information, it is fairly easy to compute the sum of the
scores, ΣX.

For example, sample 1 consists of n = 8 scores with a
mean of $\overline{X} = 12$. You can find ΣX for the scores by using the
formula for the mean, and substituting the two values that you
know,

$$\overline{X} = \frac{\Sigma X}{n}$$

In this case,

$$12 = \frac{\Sigma X}{8}$$

Multiplying both sides of the equation by 8 gives,

$$8(12) = \Sigma X$$
$$96 = \Sigma X$$

Often this process is easier to understand if you put
dollar-signs on the numbers and remember that the mean is the
amount that each individual receives if the total is divided
equally. For this example, we have a group of 8 people (n)
who have \$14 each ($\overline{X}$). If the group puts all their money
together (ΣX), how much will they have? Again the answer is
$\Sigma X = \$96$.

Step 2: Repeat the process in Step 1 for each individual data set. If the problem involves adding a single score to an existing data set, then you can treat the single score as a sample with $n = 1$ and $X = \bar{X} = \Sigma X$.

For this example, Sample 2 has a $n = 5$ and $\Sigma X = 45$, and Sample 3 has $n = 1$ and $\Sigma X = 4$.

Step 3: Once you have determined n and ΣX for each individual data set, then you simply add the individual ns to find the number of scores in the combined set. In the same way, you simply add the ΣXs to find the overall sum of the scores in the combined data set. For this example,

combined n = $8 + 5 + 1 = 14$
combined ΣX = $96 + 45 + 4 = 145$

Step 4: Finally you compute the mean for the combined group using the standard formula for $\bar{X}$.

$$\bar{X} = \frac{\Sigma X}{n} = 145/14 = 10.36$$

HINTS AND CAUTIONS

1. One of the most common errors in computing central tendency occurs when students are attempting to find the mean for data in a frequency distribution table. You must remember that the frequency distribution table condenses a large set of scores into a concise, organized distribution; the table does not list each of the individual scores. One way of avoiding confusion is to transform the frequency distribution table back into the original list of scores. For example, the following frequency distribution table presents a distribution for which three individuals had scores of $X = 5$; one individual had $X = 4$; four individuals had $X = 3$; no one

had X = 2; and two individuals had X = 1. When each of these scores is listed individually, it is much easier to see that N = 10 and $\Sigma X = 33$ for these data.

Frequency Distribution		Original X Values
X	f	5
5	3	5
4	1	5
3	4	4
2	0	3
1	2	3
		3
		3
		1
		1

2. Many students incorrectly assume that the median corresponds to the midpoint of the range of scores. For example, it is tempting to say that the median for a 100-point test would be X = 50. Be careful! The correct interpretation is that the median divides the set of scores (or individuals) into two equal groups. On a 100-point test, for example, the median could be X = 95 if the test was very easy and 50% of the class scored above 95. You must know where the individual scores are located before you can find the median.

For simple distributions it often is easy to locate the median if you first sketch a histogram of the frequency distribution. If each score is represented by a "block" in the graph, you can find the median by positioning a vertical line so that it divides the blocks into two equal piles.

1.   Central Tendency is probably the most commonly used technique in the entire field of descriptive statistics. Define the general purpose of central tendency.

2.   In this chapter we identified three different procedures for measuring central tendency: the mean, the median, and the mode.   Briefly explain why three different measures are necessary - why is one standard procedure not sufficient?

3.   The primary measure of central tendency is the mean.
   a.   In words, explain how the mean is computed.
   b.   Identify the symbol and formula used for a population mean and for a sample mean.

4.   When data are organized in a frequency distribution table, you must be careful to use all of the information in the table (X and f values) to find the mean.   The number of scores (N) can be found by summing the frequencies: $N = \Sigma f$.   To find the sum of the scores (ΣX) you must be careful to include all N scores.   You can either list all the scores individually and then add them, or you can multiply each score by its frequency and sum these products;
   $$\text{sum of scores} = \Sigma fX$$

Find N, ΣX, and μ for the set of scores in the following frequency distribution table.

X	f
5	2
4	1
3	4
2	3
1	2

5.   Occasionally a researcher will transform a set of data by adding a constant to each score, or multiplying each score by a constant. The mean will be affected by these transformations. It is easy to determine exactly how the mean is affected if you simply remember that the mean is the "average score." Whatever is done to the other scores is also done to the mean.

   a.   If 10 points are added to each score in a population with μ = 80, the new population will have a mean of _____ .

   b.   For a population with μ = 30, if each score is multiplied by 4 the resulting population will have a mean of _____ .

6.   The formula for the mean establishes a relationship between the sum (ΣX), the number of scores (n), and the mean ($\overline{X}$). Whenever two of these three values are known, you should be able to find the third. It may help you to remember this relationship if you think of the mean as the amount that each individual would get if the total (ΣX) were divided equally among the number of individuals (N) in the group.

   a.   If a sample of n = 8 scores has a mean of $\overline{X}$ = 6, the total for this group must be ΣX = _____ .

b.   A sample has $\Sigma X = 100$ and a mean of $\overline{X} = 20$.   How many individuals are in the sample?

7.   When two separate sets of scores are combined you can find the mean for the total group by computing the weighted mean.   To find the weighted mean, you simply remember the definition of the mean:

the mean = (sum of scores)/(number of scores)

To find the sum of scores for the combined group, you first must find ΣX for each of the separate groups and then add the two sums together.   To find the number of scores in the combined group, you just add the number of scores in the first group and the number in the second group.
    a.   If one group of scores has $n = 7$ and $\overline{X} = 2$, and a second group has $n = 3$ and $\overline{X} = 12$, then the combined group will have $n =$ _____ and $\Sigma X =$ _____.   The mean for this combined group would be $\overline{X} =$ _____.
    b.   A sample of $n = 9$ scores has $\overline{X} = 7$.   If an extra score of $X = 4$ is added to this sample, what is the value of the new mean?

8.   Although the mean is the most common measure of central tendency, there are circumstances where the mean does not provide a good measure of central tendency or where the mean simply cannot be computed.   In these situations you can use either the median or the mode as an alternative to the mean.
    a.   Define the median.
    b.   Define the mode.

9. For each of the following situations explain why the mean is not appropriate and identify the best alternative measure of central tendency.

   a. A skewed distribution with a few extreme scores.

   b. A distribution of scores measured on a nominal scale.

   c. An open-ended distribution

10. Compute the mean, median, and mode for the following set of scores.

Scores: 5, 7, 5, 4, 3, 12, 9, 6, 6, 5, 7, 5, 6, 4

11. Compute the mean, median, and mode for the set of scores shown in the following frequency distribution table.

X	f
7	1
6	1
5	1
4	1
3	4
2	3
1	1

12. One value of central tendency is that it allows a researcher to compare two different sets of scores. Suppose a researcher is evaluating a "new and improved" formula for cat food. A sample of twenty cats is obtained and each cat is deprived of food for 12 hours prior to testing. In the test, each cat is given free access to two bowls of cat food. One bowl contains the new improved food and the other bowl contains the regular

food. The researcher records the amount of food eaten
from each bowl in a one-hour period. The data are as
follows:

New Improved Food					Regular Food			
8	3	5	7		3	4	1	7
10	9	2	8		7	4	8	5
6	4	2	8		1	11	3	6
9	12	7	9		2	3	7	5
11	8	3	7		4	2	6	4

    a. Compute the mean amount eaten for each type of cat
food.

    b. Does it appear that the cats have a preference for
the new improved formula?

ANSWERS TO SELF-TEST

1. The purpose of central tendency is to find a single
value that best represents an entire distribution of
scores.

2. No single procedure for measuring central tendency
always provides a good representative value. For
example, the mean can be displaced by extreme scores in a
distribution so that it is not a representative score.
Also, there are situations where the mean cannot be
calculated (for example, with open-ended distributions,
undetermined scores, or data measured on a nominal
scale). Thus, there are three different measures of
central tendency that are intended to be used in

different situations. Usually, at least one of these measures will provide a good representative value for the distribution.

3. a. The mean is obtained by adding the scores to find the total, then dividing the total by the number of scores.

   b. The population mean is identified by μ, the Greek letter mu.

$$\mu = \frac{\Sigma X}{N}$$

The sample mean for a set of X values is identified by the symbol $\overline{X}$ ("X bar").

$$\overline{X} = \frac{\Sigma X}{n}$$

4. $N = \Sigma f = 12$. The 12 scores add to $\Sigma X = 34$, and the mean is $\mu = 34/12 = 2.83$.

5. a. The new mean is 90.
   b. The new mean is 120.

6. a. The 8 scores must sum to $\Sigma X = 48$.
   b. If a set of scores totals 100 and averages 20, there must be $n = 5$ scores.

7. a. For the first group, $n = 7$, $\overline{X} = 2$ and $\Sigma X = 14$. The second group has $n = 3$, $\overline{X} = 12$, and $\Sigma X = 36$. For the combined group, $n = 10$ and $\Sigma X = 50$. The combined group has a mean of $50/10 = 5$.

   b. The original set of $n = 9$ scores totals $\Sigma X = 63$. When the new score is added, $n = 10$ and $\Sigma X = 67$, so the new mean is $67/10 = 6.7$.

8.   a.   The median is the score that divides the distribution exactly in half. Exactly 50% of the scores in the distribution have values equal to or less than the median.

     b.   The mode is the score with the greatest frequency.

9.   a.   In a skewed distribution the extreme scores will displace the mean toward the tail. In this case the median provides a more centrally located value.

     b.   With data from a nominal scale you cannot compute a mean or a median. In this case you must use the mode.

     c.   With an open-ended distribution you cannot compute the mean. The median is the best measure of central tendency in this situation.

10. The mean is 84/14 = 6.00. The median is X = 5.5, and the mode is X = 5.

11. The mean is 41/12 = 3.42. The median is X = 3.00, and the Mode is X = 3.

12. a.   The mean for the new improved food is $\bar{X}$ = 6.90. For the regular food, the mean is $\bar{X}$ = 4.65.

     b.   It appears that the cats prefer the new formula. On average, they ate nearly 50% more of the new food than of the regular food.

CHAPTER 4 VARIABILITY

LEARNING OBJECTIVES

1.   Understand the measures of variability and be able to tell the difference between sets of scores with low versus high variability.

2.   Know how to calculate SS using either the computational or definitional formula.

3.   Be able to calculate the population and sample variance and standard deviation, and understand the correction used in the formulas for the sample statistics.

4.   Be familiar with the characteristics of measures of variability, especially those for standard deviation.

NEW TERMS AND CONCEPTS

The following terms were introduced in this chapter. Define or describe each term and, where appropriate, describe how each term is related to other terms in the list.

variability
range
first quartile
third quartile
semi-interquartile range
deviation score
average deviation
population variance
population variance
population standard deviation
sample variance
sample standard deviation
unbiased estimate
degrees of freedom

NEW FORMULAS

semi-interquartile range $= \dfrac{Q3 - Q1}{2}$

deviation score $= X - \mu$ or for a sample $X - \overline{X}$

$SS = \Sigma(X - \mu)^2$ or for a sample, $SS = \Sigma(X - \overline{X})^2$

$SS = \Sigma X^2 - \dfrac{(\Sigma X)^2}{N}$ or for a sample, $SS = \Sigma X^2 - \dfrac{(\Sigma X)^2}{n}$

$\sigma^2 = \dfrac{SS}{N}$ $\qquad\qquad s = \dfrac{SS}{n-1}$

$\sigma = \sqrt{\dfrac{SS}{N}}$ $\qquad\qquad s = \sqrt{\dfrac{SS}{n-1}}$

SS, Variance, and Standard Deviation: The following set
of data will be used to demonstrate the calculation of SS,
variance, and standard deviation.

Scores: 5, 3, 2, 4, 1

Step 1:   Before you begin any calculation, simply look
at the set of scores and make a preliminary estimate of
the mean and standard deviation. For this set of data,
it should be obvious that the mean is around 3, and most
of the scores are within one or two points of the mean.
Therefore, the standard deviation (standard distance from
the mean) should be about 1 or 2.

Step 2:   Determine which formula you will use to compute
SS. If you have a relatively small set of data and the
mean is a whole number, then use the definitional
formula. Otherwise, the computational formula is a
better choice. For this example there are only 5 scores
and the mean is equal to 3. The definitional formula
would be fine for these scores.

Step 3:   Calculate SS. Note that it does not matter
whether the set of scores is a sample or a population
when you are computing SS. For this example, we will use
formulas with population notation, but using sample
notation would not change the result.

Definitional Formula: List each score in a column.
In a second column put the deviation score for each
X value. (Check that the deviations add to zero).
In a third column list the squared deviation scores.
Then simply add the values in the third column.

X	$(X - \mu)$	$(X - \mu)^2$
5	2	4
3	0	0
2	-1	1
4	1	1
1	-2	4
	0	10 = SS

Computational Formula: List each score in a column. In second column list the squared value for each X. Then find the sum for each column. These are the two sums that are needed for the computational formula.

X	X^2
5	25
3	9
2	4
4	16
1	1
15	55

$$\Sigma X = 15$$

$$\Sigma X^2 = 55$$

Then use the two sums in the computational formula to calculate SS.

$$SS = \Sigma X^2 - \frac{(\Sigma X)^2}{N}$$

$$= 55 - \frac{(15)^2}{5}$$

$$= 55 - 45$$

$$= 10$$

Step 4: Now you must determine whether the set of scores is a sample or a population. With a population you use N in the formulas for variance and standard deviation. With a sample, use n - 1.

For a Population	For a Sample
$\sigma^2 = \dfrac{SS}{N} = \dfrac{10}{5} = 2$	$s^2 = \dfrac{SS}{n-1} = \dfrac{10}{4} = 2.5$
$\sigma = \sqrt{\dfrac{SS}{N}} = \sqrt{2} = 1.41$	$s = \sqrt{\dfrac{SS}{n-1}} = \sqrt{2.5} = 1.58$

HINTS AND CAUTIONS

1. Mistakes are commonly made in the computational formula for SS. Often, ΣX^2 is confused with (ΣX^2). The ΣX^2 indicates that the X values are first squared, then summed. On the other hand, $(\Sigma X)^2$ requires that the X values are first added, then the sum is squared.

2. Remember, it is impossible to get a negative value for SS because, by definition, SS is the sum of the squared deviation scores. The squaring operation eliminates all of the negative signs.

3. The computational formula is usually easier to use than the definitional formula because the mean usually is not a whole number.

4. When computing a variance of a standard deviation, be sure to check whether you are computing the measure for a population or a sample. Remember, the sample

variance and standard deviation use n - 1 in the
denominator so that these values will provide unbiased
estimates of the corresponding population parameters.

5.   Note that you do not use n - 1 in the formula for
sample SS. The value n - 1 is used to compute sample
variance and standard deviation _after_ you have calculated
SS.

SELF-TEST AND REVIEW

1.   In this chapter we identified four measures of
variability: the range, the semi-interquartile range,
variance, and standard deviation.
      a.   Define the basic purpose of a measure of
variability.
      b.   In words, define each of the four measures.

2.   In Chapter 3 we noted that the mean is the most
commonly used measure of central tendency. Partly
because variance and standard deviation are directly
related to the mean, these two values are the most common
measures of variability. Explain how variance and
standard deviation are related to the mean.

3.   The definitions (and calculations) for variance and
standard deviation begin with the concept of a deviation
score.
      a.   What information is given by the sign (+ or -)
of a deviation score?
      b.   What information is given by the numerical value
of a deviation score?

c. In a distribution with $\mu = 80$, you have a deviation score of -3. What is your score?

d. For any distribution of scores, what value is always obtained for the sum of the deviation scores?

4. To compute either variance or standard deviation, you first must find the sum of the squared deviation scores - also called the <u>sums of squares</u> or simply SS. For the following set of scores, 5, 2, 8, 3

a. Compute SS with the computational formula.

b. Compute SS with the definitional formula.

c. Which formula is better suited for these data? Why?

d. Does the value you obtain for SS depend on whether these scores are a sample or a population?

5. Population variance is defined as the average squared deviation. Population standard deviation is the square root of the variance, and describes the standard distance from the mean for a population of scores.

a. Explain how the formula for population variance is directly related to the definition.

b. By just looking at the following data, estimate the variance and standard deviation for this population of scores, 3, 3, 6, 8, 2, 6, 7, 5.

c. Calculate the variance and standard deviation for the population in part b.

6. Although a sample mean provides a good estimate of its population mean, sample variability tends to be biased.

a. Explain what is meant by "biased."

b. How is sample variability biased? (Is it too large or too small?)

c. How is this bias corrected in the formula for sample variance and sample standard deviation?

7. Calculate SS, variance, and standard deviation for the following sample of scores, 15, 16, 9, 1, 9.

8. If you think of standard deviation as a measure of distance, it is easier to determine how the standard deviation will be affected by various transformations of scale.

a. What happens to the distance between two individual scores if a constant amount is added to every score in a distribution?

b. What happens to the standard deviation if a constant amount is added to every score in a distribution?

c. What happens to the distance between two individual scores if every score in the distribution is multiplied by a constant?

d. What happens to the standard deviation if every score in a distribution is multiplied by a constant?

ANSWERS TO SELF-TEST

1. a. The purpose of a measure of variability is to describe how spread out the scores are in a distribution.

b. The range measures the distance from the largest to the smallest score. The semi-interquartile range measures one-half the distance from the first quartile to the third quartile. (That is, one-half the range covered by the middle 50% of the distribution.) Variance is the average squared deviation. Standard deviation is the square root of the variance and measures the standard distance between a score and the mean.

2. Variance and standard deviation are based on deviation scores which measure the distance between each score and the mean.

3. a. The sign of a deviation score tells whether the score is above (+) or below (-) the mean.

b. The numerical value of a deviation score tells the distance (number of points) between the score and the mean.

c. A deviation of -3 corresponds to X = 77.

d. The deviation scores always sum to zero.

4. a. With the computational formula $\Sigma X = 18$ and $\Sigma X^2 = 102$. SS = 21.

b. The mean for the scores is 4.5, and the deviation scores are 0.5, -2.5, 3.5, and -1.5. The sum of squared deviations is SS = 21.

c. The computational formula is better because the mean is not a whole number.

d. No. The value obtained for SS is not influenced by whether the data are a sample or a population.

5. a. Variance is the average squared deviation. To find this "average," you divide the <u>sum</u> of the squared deviations by the <u>number</u> of squared deviations.

b. The mean appears to be about 5 and the individual scores are generally about 2 points away from the mean. Estimate the standard deviation to be 2 and the variance to be 4.

c. SS = 32, variance = 4, and standard deviation = 2.

6. a. A sample statistic that, on average, either underestimates or overestimates its corresponding population parameter is said to be biased.

b. On average, sample variability underestimates population variability. It is too small.

c. The bias in sample variability is corrected by using n - 1 in the formulas for variance and standard deviation. Dividing by a smaller number (n - 1 instead of n) increases the values obtained for the sample.

7. SS = 144, s^2 = 36, and s = 6

8. a. If a constant is added to each score, the distance between two scores is not changed.

b. When a constant is added to every score in a distribution, the standard deviation is not changed.

c. If each score is multiplied by a constant, the distance between two scores also is multiplied by the constant.

d. When every score in a distribution is multiplied by a constant, the standard deviation is multiplied by the same constant.

CHAPTER **5** Z–SCORES: LOCATION OF SCORES AND
                      STANDARDIZED DISTRIBUTIONS

LEARNING OBJECTIVES

1.   You should be able to describe and understand the
purpose for z-scores.

2.   You should be able to transform X values into z-
scores or to transform z-scores into X values.

3.   You should be able to describe the effects of
standardizing a distribution by transforming the entire
set of raw scores into z-scores.

4. By using z-scores you should be able to transform any set of scores into a distribution with a predetermined mean and standard deviation.

NEW TERMS AND CONCEPTS

The following terms were introduced in this chapter. Define or describe each term and, where appropriate, describe how each term is related to other terms in the list.

raw score
z-score
standardized distribution

NEW FORMULAS

$$z = \frac{X - \mu}{\sigma}$$

$$z\sigma = X - \mu = \text{deviation}$$

$$X = \mu + z\sigma$$

STEP-BY-STEP

Changing X to z: The process of changing an X value to a z-score involves finding the precise location of X within its distribution. We will begin with a distribution with $\mu = 60$ and $\sigma = 12$. The goal is to find the z-score for X = 75.

Step 1: First determine whether X is above or below the mean. This will determine the sign of the z-score. For

our example, X is above μ so the z-score will be
positive.

Step 2:   Next, find the distance between X and μ. For
our example,

$$X - \mu = 75 - 60 = 15 \text{ points}$$

Note: Steps 1 and 2 simply determine a deviation score
(sign and magnitude). If you are using the z-score
formula, these two steps correspond to the numerator of
the equation.

Step 3:   Convert the distance from Step 2 into standard
deviation units. In the z-score equation, this step
corresponds to dividing by σ. For this example,

$$15/12 = 1.25$$

If you are using the z-score definition (rather than the
formula), you simply compare the magnitude of the
distance (Step 2) with the magnitude of the standard
deviation. For this example, our distance of 15 points
is equal to one standard deviation plus 3 or more points.
The extra 3 points are equal to one-quarter of a standard
deviation, so the total distance is one and one-quarter
standard deviations.

Step 4:   Combine the sign from Step 1 with the number of
standard deviations you obtained in Step 3. For this
example,

$$z = +1.25$$

Changing z to X: The process of converting a z-score into an
X value corresponds to finding the score that is located at a
specified position in a distribution. Again, suppose we

have a population with $\mu = 60$ and $\sigma = 12$. What is the X value corresponding to z = -0.50?

Step 1: The sign of the z-score tells whether X is above or below the mean. For this example, the X value we want is below μ.

Step 2: The magnitude of the z-score tells how many standard deviations there are between X and μ. For this example, the distance is one-half a standard deviation which is (1/2)(12) = 6 points.

Step 3: Starting with the value of the mean, use the direction (Step 1) and the distance (Step 2) to determine the X value. For this example, we want to find the score that is 6 points below $\mu = 60$. Therefore,
$$X = 60 - 6 = 54$$

HINTS AND CAUTIONS

1. Rather than memorizing formulas for z-scores, we suggest that you rely on the definition of a z-score. Remember a z-score identifies a location by specifying the direction from the mean (+ or -) and the distance from the mean in terms of standard deviations.

2. When transforming scores from X to z (or from z to X) it is wise to check your answer by reversing the transformation. For example, given a population with $\mu = 54$ and $\sigma = 4$ a score of X = 46 corresponds to a z-score of

$$z = \frac{X - \mu}{\sigma} = \frac{46 - 54}{4} = \frac{-8}{4} = -2.00$$

To check this answer, begin with the z-score and convert it back into an X value. In this case, z = -2.00 specifies a score that is located below the mean by 2 standard deviations. This distance is

$$z\sigma = -2.00(4) = -8 \text{ points}$$

With a mean of $\mu = 54$, the score must be

$$X = 54 - 8 = 46.$$

SELF-TEST AND REVIEW

1.   Describe the general purpose of a z-score.

2.   A z-score has two parts: the sign and the number. Describe the information provided by each of these parts.

3.   For a population with $\mu = 90$ and $\sigma = 25$ find the z-score corresponding to each of the following X values.

   a.   X = 95
   b.   X = 110
   c.   X = 65
   d.   X = 80

4.   For a population with $\mu = 60$ and $\sigma = 6$ find the X value corresponding to each of the following z-scores.

   a.   z = +1.50
   b.   z = -0.50
   c.   z = +2.00
   d.   z = -0.33

5.   The z-score formula is useful not only for computing z-scores, but also for establishing a relationship among the z-score location, the individual score at that location, the population mean, and the population

standard deviation. If you are given any three of these values, you should be able to determine the fourth.

    a.   In a population with $\mu = 80$, and a score of $X = 88$ corresponds to $z = +2.00$. What is the standard deviation for this population?

    b.   In a population with $\sigma = 12$, a score of $X = 64$ corresponds to a z-score of -0.25. What is the mean for this population?

    c.   For a population with $\mu = 40$ and $\sigma = 10$, what is the score corresponding to $z = +1.50$?

    d.   For a population with $\mu = 75$ and $\sigma = 8$, what is the z-score corresponding to $X = 63$?

6.   A z-score indicates a relative position within a distribution - that is, it tells where a particular score is located <u>relative</u> to the other scores in the distribution. If the results from a test were reported as z-scores and you obtained $z = -2.00$, does that indicate that your performance on the test was very poor? Explain your answer.

7.   On an exam with $\mu = 70$ and $\sigma = 10$, you have a score of $X = 85$.

    a.   What is your z-score on this exam?

    b.   If the instructor added 5 points to every score, what would happen to your z-score? (Hint: What would happen to your position relative to the other scores in the class?)

    c.   If the instructor multiplied every score by 2, what would happen to your z-score?

8.   When an entire distribution is transformed into z-scores, the result is a standardized distribution of z-scores.

a. What is the mean for this standardized distribution?

b. What is the standard deviation for this standardized distribution?

c. How does the shape of the standardized distribution compare with the shape of the original population?

9. You can use z-scores to transform any population into a standardized distribution with a predetermined mean and standard deviation. To determine how this kind of transformation will affect any individual score, you first compute the z-score (location) in the original population. Then you use the new mean and standard deviation to determine precisely the same location (z-score) in the new distribution. Thus, each individual score has exactly the same location in the original population and in the transformed distribution. This process can be expressed as a formula:

$$\text{new } X = z(\text{new } \sigma) + \text{new } \mu$$

Suppose we begin with a population with $\mu = 48$ and $\sigma = 8$. This population is transformed into a standardized distribution with $\mu = 100$ and $\sigma = 20$. Find the transformed value for each of the following scores from the original population.

a. X = 48
b. X = 50
c. X = 44
d. X = 32

10. By standardizing two different distributions so that they have the same mean and standard deviation, it is possible to compare individual scores even though they

originally came from different distributions. Suppose we are examining the physical development of two children. Tom is 39 inches tall. For his age group, the population average height is 36 inches with $\sigma = 2$. Henry is 46 inches tall at an age when the population average height is $\mu = 44$ with $\sigma = 3$. Which child is taller relative to other children his own age?

ANSWERS TO PROBLEMS

1. The purpose of a z-score is to provide a single value that specifies a precise location within a distribution.

2. A positive z-score indicates a position above the mean. A negative z-score corresponds to a value below the mean. The numerical value of a z-score indicates distance from the mean by measuring the number of standard deviations between X and μ.

3. a. $z = +0.20$
    b. $z = +0.80$
    c. $z = -1.00$
    d. $z = -0.40$

4. a. $X = 69$
    b. $X = 57$
    c. $X = 72$
    d. $X = 58$

5. a. The score is 8 points above the mean and is located 2 standard deviations above the mean. Therefore $\sigma = 4$.

   b. The score is located below the mean by a quarter of a standard deviation, which corresponds to 3 points below the mean. Therefore $\mu = 67$.

   c. The score is above the mean by one and one-half standard deviations, which corresponds to 15 points above the mean. The score is X = 55.

   d. The score is below the mean by 12 points, which corresponds to one and one-half standard deviations below the mean. The z-score is z = -1.50.

6. The z-score indicates that your performance was very poor relative to the rest of the class. Although you may have done quite well on the exam (for example 90% correct), most of the class had scores higher than yours.

7. a. z = +1.50.

   b. Adding a constant does not change your position within the distribution. Your z-score is still +1.50.

   c. Your z-score is still +1.50. Although your score is multiplied, the mean and standard deviation also are multiplied. The result is that you are still located above the mean by 1.5 standard deviations.

8. a. When a distribution is transformed into z-scores, the mean becomes zero.

   b. When a distribution is transformed into z-scores, the standard deviation becomes one.

   c. Transforming X values into z-scores does not change the shape of the distribution.

9.   a.   X = 48 corresponds to z = 0.   In the new distribution this location corresponds to X = 100.

    b.   X = 50 corresponds to z = +0.25 which corresponds to X = 105 in the new distribution.

    c.   X = 44 corresponds to z = -.50.   X = 90 in the new distribution.

    d.   X = 32 corresponds to z = -2.00.   X = 60 in the new distribution.

10.   Tom has a z-score of z = +1.50.   Henry has a z-score of z = +0.67.   Tom has shown greater development relative to other children his own age.

CHAPTER **6** PROBABILITY

LEARNING OBJECTIVES

1.   Know how to determine the probability of an event.

2.   Know when and how to use the addition and
multiplication rules for probability.

3.   Be able to use the unit normal table to determine
the probabilities for events that are normally
distributed.

4.   Be able to use the normal approximation to compute
probabilities for a binomial distribution.

NEW TERMS AND CONCEPTS

The following terms were introduced in this chapter. Define or describe each term and, where appropriate, describe how each term is related to other terms in the list.

probability
proportion
random sample
sampling with replacement
addition rule
mutually exclusive events
multiplication rule
independent events
normal distribution
unit normal table
binomial distribution
normal approximation to the binomial

NEW FORMULAS

$$P(A) = \frac{\text{number of outcomes classified as A}}{\text{total number of possible outcomes}}$$

$$P(A \text{ or } B) = P(A) + P(B) - P(A \text{ and } B \text{ together})$$

$$P(A \text{ and } B) = P(A) \times P(B)$$

$$z = \frac{X - pn}{\sqrt{npq}} \quad \text{(binomial)}$$

Finding the probability associated with a specified score. The general process involves converting the score (X) into a z-score, then using the unit normal table to find the probability associated with the z-score. We will use the following example to look at the details of the process.

For a normal distribution with $\mu = 100$ and $\sigma = 10$, find the probability of randomly selecting a score greater than 95.

Step 1: Sketch the distribution and identify the mean and standard deviation.

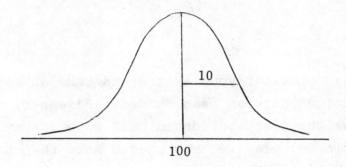

Step 2: Find the approximate location of the specified score and draw a vertical line through the distribution. For this example, X = 95 is located below the mean by roughly one-half of the standard deviation.

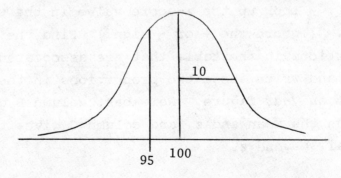

Step 3: Read the problem again to determine whether you want the proportion greater than the score (right of your line) or less than the score (left of the line). Then shade in the appropriate portion of the distribution. For this example we want the proportion consisting of scores greater than 95, so shade in the portion to the right of X = 95.

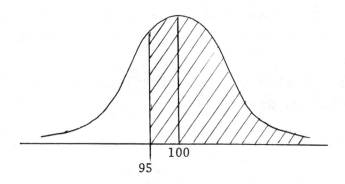

Step 4: Look at your sketch and make an estimate of the proportion that has been shaded. Remember, the mean divides the distribution in half with 50% on each side. For this example, we have shaded more than 50% of the distribution. The shaded area appears to be about 60% or 70% of the distribution.

Step 5: Transform the X value into a z-score. For this example, X = 95 corresponds to z = -0.50.

Step 6: Look up the z-score value in the unit normal table. (Ignore the + or - sign.) Find the two proportions in the table that are associated with your z-score and write these two proportions in the appropriate places on your figure. Remember, column B gives the area between the mean and z, and column C gives the area in the tail beyond z.

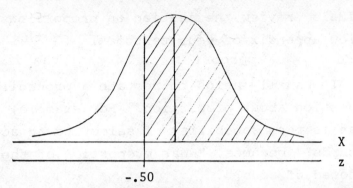

-.50

<u>Step</u> <u>7</u>:   If one of the proportions from the table
corresponds exactly with the shaded area of your figure
then you are done. Otherwise, you will need to do some
additional arithmetic to get the final answer. Usually,
this arithmetic involves adding 50% (.5000) to one of the
proportions from the table. (Remember, exactly 50% of
the distribution is on each side of the mean.) For this
example, the column B proportion, .1915, corresponds to
part of the shaded area. To find the total shaded area
you must add the 50% located on the right-hand side of
the mean. Thus our final answer is

P(X > 95) = .1915 + .5000 = .6915

<u>Step</u> <u>8</u>: Compare your final answer with the estimate you
made in Step 4. If your answer is not in agreement with
your preliminary estimate, re-work the problem.

HINTS AND CAUTIONS

1.   In using probability, you should be comfortable in
converting fractions into decimals or percentages. These
values all represent ways of expressing portions of the

whole.   if you have difficulty with fractions or
decimals, review the section on proportions in the math
review appendix of your textbook.

2.   It usually helps to restate a probability problem as
a question about proportion. For example, the problem,
"What is the probability of selecting an ace from a deck
of cards?" becomes, "What proportion of the deck is
composed of aces?"

3.   When using the unit normal table to answer
probability questions, you should always start by
sketching a normal distribution and shading in the area
of the distribution for which you need a proportion.

4.   When you are computing probabilities for a binomial
distribution remember to use the real limits for each
score. For example, a score of X = 18 actually
corresponds to an interval from 17.5 to 18.5. Also,
scores greater than 18 begin at the upper real limit of
18.5.

SELF-TEST AND REVIEW

1.   If a situation has several possible outcomes, A, B,
C, D, etc., what is the definition of the probability
that event A will occur?

2.   The definition of probability requires <u>random
sampling</u>. Identify the two requirements that must be met
for random sampling.

3. Define "sampling with replacement" and "sampling without replacement." Which of these sampling methods is necessary for a random sample.

4. In this chapter we identified two rules for determining the probability associated with combinations of events. If A and B are two events, the first rule determines the probability that either A or B will occur. The second rule determines the probability that both A and B will occur. Identify these two probability rules by completing the following formulas.

    a. P(A or B) =

    b. P(A and B) =

5. A car rental agency has a fleet of 50 domestic and 30 foreign cars. For the domestic cars, 18 are luxury models and the remainder are standard-equipment sedans. For the foreign cars, 16 are luxury and the remainder are standard models. If the cars are assigned to customers randomly, what are the following probabilities?

    a. P(foreign luxury car)

    b. P(standard model)

    c. P(foreign or luxury model)

6. The probability definition that we are using equates probability and proportion. When you are determining probability for a distribution of scores, a specific probability can be visualized as a specific proportion or area of the distribution graph. For normal distributions, the proportion of area can be determined by consulting the unit normal table. Use this table to answer the following questions. Assume a normal distribution for each question.

a. What is the probability of obtaining a z-score greater than 1.25?

b. What is the probability of obtaining a z-score less than 0.50?

c. What proportion of the distribution consists of z-scores greater than -1.00?

d. $P(z > 2.00) = $?

e. $P(z < -.50) = $?

7. The unit normal table lists z-scores and the corresponding proportions for the normal distribution. If you know a specific z-score, you can look up the corresponding proportion. In the same way, if you know a specific proportion, you can look up the corresponding z-score. Find the z-score that separates a normal distribution into the following two portions:

   a. lowest 75% versus highest 25%
   b. lowest 90% versus highest 10%
   c. lowest 35% versus highest 65%
   d. lowest 42% versus highest 58%

8. The value of the unit normal table comes from the fact that any normal distribution becomes a unit normal distribution when you transform the X values into z-scores. Thus, the unit normal table can be used to find probabilities for any normal distribution, provided that you first change from X to z. Find the following probabilities for a normal distribution with $\mu = 80$ and $\sigma = 12$.

   a. $P(X > 86)$
   b. $P(X > 77)$
   c. $P(X < 95)$
   d. $P(X < 68)$

9. In Chapter 5 you learned how to transform X values into z-scores, or transform z-scores into X values. Now, the unit normal table allows you to find the probability corresponding to any z-score, or to find the z-score corresponding to any probability. By combining these two processes, it is possible to find the probability associated with a specific score: first convert the X value to a z-score, then use the unit normal table to look up the probability.

X -----> z ------> Probability

You also should be able to start with a specific probability (or proportion) and find the corresponding X value: first use the unit normal table to find the z-score, then transform the z-score into an X value.

Probability -----> z -----> X

For a normal distribution with μ = 80 and σ = 12, find the X value associated with each of the following proportions:

a. What X value separates the distribution into the top 40% versus the bottom 60%?

b. What is the minimum X value needed to be in the top 25% of the distribution?

c. What X value separates the top 60% from the bottom 40% of the distribution?

10. When you are solving probability problems with normal distributions, you should always sketch a distribution, locate the mean and standard deviation, and shade in the portion specified in the problem. Also, remember that the unit normal table contains only limited information. For example, the table shows only positive z-scores and it only lists two proportions associated with each z-score. For each of the following problems

you cannot find the answer directly in the table. But
the information in the table can be combined with a
little thinking to lead you to the final answer.

a.   For a normal distribution with $\mu = 60$ and $\sigma = 5$,
what is the probability of randomly selecting a score
between 61 and 65?

b.   For a normal distribution with $\mu = 60$ and $\sigma = 5$,
what is the probability of randomly selecting a score
between 57 and 62?

11. Now for some "trick" questions. I will warn you
that the answers to these questions are not in the unit
normal table.

a.   For a positively skewed distribution with $\mu = 80$
and $\sigma = 10$, what is the probability of randomly selecting
a score less than 75?

b.   For a normal distribution with $\mu = 40$ and $\sigma = 8$,
what is the probability of selecting a score that is
greater than 42 and less than 38?

12. The binomial distribution is used in situations
where each individual in a population can be classified
into one of two categories. The two categories are
identified as A and B with probabilities, $P(A) = p$ and
$P(B) = q$. The binomial distribution shows the
probability of X occurrences of category A in a series of
n events. When both pn and qn are at least 10, the
binomial distribution is approximated by a normal
distribution with $\mu = pn$ and $\sigma = \sqrt{npq}$. In this situation
you can use z-scores and the unit normal table to compute
binomial probabilities.

According to most estimates, 10% of the general
population are left-handed and 90% are right-handed. A
neurological theory predicts that there should be a

disproportionate number of left-handers among artists. In a sample of n = 100 artists a psychologist finds 18 are left-handed. What is the probability of obtaining more than 17 left-handed individuals in a random sample of n = 100?

ANSWERS TO SELF-TEST

1.   The probability of event A is defined as a proportion:

$$P = \frac{\text{number of outcomes classified as A}}{\text{total number of possible outcomes}}$$

2.   The two requirements for a random sample are:
     a.   Every individual in the population has an equal probability of being selected.
     b.   If more than one individual is selected, the probability of being chosen is unchanged after each selection is made.

3.   When you are sampling with replacement, each individual selected for the sample must be returned to the population before the next selection is made. Sampled individuals are not returned when you are sampling without replacement. A random sample requires sampling with replacement so that the probabilities are not changed after each selection.

4.   a.   P(A or B) = P(A) + P(B) - P(A and B together)
     b.   P(A and B) = P(A)xP(B)

5.   a.   P(foreign luxury car) = 16/80

     b.   P(standard model) = 32/80 + 14/80 = 46/80

     c.   P(foreign or luxury) = 30/80 + 34/80 - 16/80 = 48/80

6.   a.   P(z > 1.25)   =   .1056

     b.   P(z < 0.50)   =   .6915

     c.   P(z > -1.00) =   .8413

     d.   P(z > 2.00)   =   .0228

     e.   P(z < -0.50) -   .3085

7.   a.   z = 0.67

     b.   z = 1.28

     c.   z = -0.39

     d.   z = -0.20

8.   a.   z = 0.50 and p = .3085

     b.   z = -0.25 and p = .5987

     c.   z = 1.25 and p = .8944

     d.   z = -1.00 and p = .1587

9.   a.   z = 0.25 and X = 83

     b.   z = 0.67 and X = 88

     c.   z = -0.25 and X = 77

10. a.   The z-scores are 0.20 and 1.00, and p = .2620

     b.   The z-scores are -.60 and 0.40, and p = .3811

11. a.   You cannot use the unit normal table because the distribution is not normal.

     b.   It is impossible for a score to be greater than 42 and less than 38 (p = 0).

12. With n = 100 and p = 0.1, the binomial distribution will be approximately normal with $\mu = 10$ and $\sigma = 3$. Using the real limit of 17.5,

$$P(X > 17.5) = P(z > 2.50) = .0062$$

It is very unlikely to obtain this result for a random sample from the general population.

CHAPTER **7** PROBABILITY AND SAMPLES: THE DISTRIBUTION
OF SAMPLE MEANS

LEARNING OBJECTIVES

1.   For any specific sampling situation, you should be
able to define and describe the distribution of sample
means by identifying its shape, the expected value of $\bar{X}$,
and the standard error of $\bar{X}$.

2.   You should be able to define and calculate the
standard error of $\bar{X}$.

3.   You should be able to compute a z-score which
specifies the location of a particular sample mean within
the distribution of sample means.

4.   Using the distribution of sample means, you should be able to compute the probability of obtaining specific values for a sample mean obtained from a given population.

NEW TERMS AND CONCEPTS

The following terms were introduced in this chapter. Define or describe each term and, where appropriate, describe how each term is related to other terms in the list.

the distribution of sample means
sampling distribution
expected value of $\overline{X}$
standard error of $\overline{X}$
the central limit theorem

NEW FORMULAS

$$z = \frac{\overline{X} - \mu}{\sigma_{\overline{X}}} \qquad \sigma_{\overline{X}} = \frac{\sigma}{\sqrt{n}}$$

STEP-BY-STEP

Computing Probabilities for sample means: You should recall that we have defined probability as being equivalent to proportion.   Thus, the probability associated with a specific sample mean can be defined as a specific proportion of the distribution of sample means.   Because the distribution of sample means tends to be normal, you can use z-scores and the unit normal table to determine proportions or probabilities.

The following example demonstrates the details of this process.

For a normal population with $\mu = 60$ and $\sigma = 12$, what is the probability of selecting a random sample of n = 36 scores with a sample mean greater than 64?

In symbols, $P(\overline{X} > 64) = $?

Step 1: Rephrase the probability question as a proportion question. For this example, "Out of all the possible sample means for n = 36, what proportion have values greater than 64?"

Step 2: We are looking for a specific proportion of "all the possible sample means." The set of "all possible sample means" is the distribution of sample means. Therefore, the next step is to sketch the distribution. Show the expected value and standard error in your sketch. Caution: Be sure to use the standard error, not the standard deviation.

For this example, the distribution of sample means will have an expected value of $\mu = 60$, a standard error of $\sigma_{\overline{X}} = 12/\sqrt{36} = 2$, and it will be a normal distribution because the original population is normal (also because n > 30).

Caution: If the distribution of sample means is not normal, you cannot use the unit normal table to find probabilities.

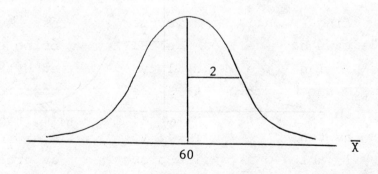

Step 3: Find the approximate location of the specified sample mean and draw a vertical line through the distribution. For this example, $\bar{X} = 64$ is located above the mean by roughly two standard deviations, or standard error.

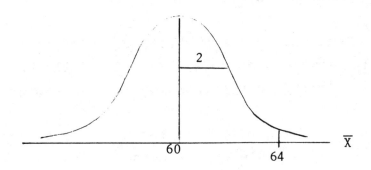

Step 4: Determine whether the problem asked for the proportion greater than or less than the specific $\bar{X}$. Then shade in the appropriate area in your sketch. For this example, we want the area greater than $\bar{X} = 64$ so shade in the area on the right-hand side of the line.

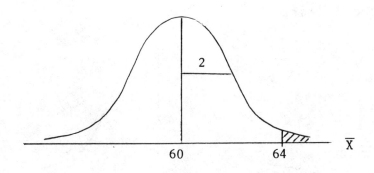

Step 5: Look at your sketch and make a preliminary estimate of the proportion that is shaded. For this example, we have shaded a very small part of the whole distribution, probably 5% or less.

Step 6: Compute the z-score for the specified sample mean. Be sure to use the z-score formula for sample means. For this example, $\overline{X} = 64$ corresponds to $z = +2.00$.

$$z = \frac{\overline{X} - \mu}{\sigma_{\overline{X}}} = \frac{64 - 60}{2} = \frac{4}{2} = 2.00$$

Step 7: Look up the z-score in the unit normal table and find the two proportions in columns B and C. For this example, the value in column C (the tail of the distribution) corresponds exactly to the proportion we want.

$$P(\overline{X} > 64) = P(z > +2.00) = .0228$$

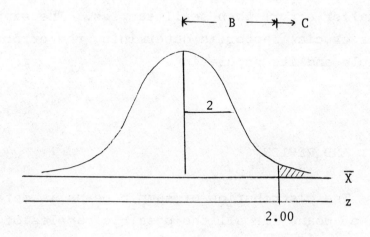

<u>Step 8</u>:   Compare your final answer with the preliminary
estimate from Step 5.   Be sure that your answer is in
agreement with the common-sense estimate you made
earlier.

HINTS AND CAUTIONS

1.   Whenever you encounter a question about a sample
mean you must remember to use the distribution of sample
means and not the original population distribution.   The
population distribution contains scores (not sample
means) and therefore should be used only when you have a
question about an individual score (n = 1).

2.   The key to working with the distribution of sample
means is the standard error of $\overline{X}$:

$$\sigma_{\overline{X}} = \frac{\sigma}{\sqrt{n}}$$

Remember, larger samples tend to be more accurate
(smaller error) than small samples.   The sample size, n,
is a crucial factor in determining the error between a
sample and its population.

SELF-TEST AND REVIEW

1.   The distribution of sample means is defined as the
set of means for all the possible samples of a specified
size (n) that can be obtained from a given population.
The distribution of sample means is an example of a

sampling distribution.   Explain what is meant by
sampling distribution.

2.   The parameters of the distribution of sample means
are specified in an important mathematical proposition
known as the Central Limit Theorem.   This theorem
identifies the three basic characteristics that describe
any distribution: Shape, Central Tendency, and
Variability.   Describe each of these three
characteristics for the distribution of sample means.

3.   The mean of the distribution of sample means is
called the expected value of $\bar{X}$.   The standard deviation
of the distribution of sample means is called the
standard error of $\bar{X}$.
       a.   If samples of size n = 25 are selected from a
population with μ = 80 and σ = 10, then the expected
value of $\bar{X}$ would be _____ and the standard error of $\bar{X}$
would be _____.
       b.   For a population with μ = 80 and σ = 10, the
distribution of sample means based on n = 4 would have an
expected value of _____ and a standard error of _____.
       c.   If the distribution of sample means for n = 9
has a standard error of 3, what is the standard deviation
of the population from which the samples were selected?

4.   In words, explain the meaning of standard error.
Remember, standard error provides a measure of distance.

5.   The location of each $\bar{X}$ in the distribution of sample
means can be identified by computing a z-score.   A z-
score value near zero indicates that the sample mean is
relatively close to the population mean.   A large z-
score (for example +2 or -2) indicates that the sample

mean is relatively far from the population mean. Find
the z-score for each of the following sample means. Each
sample was obtained from a population with μ = 100 and
σ = 10.

    a. $\overline{X}$ = 90 for a sample of n = 4
    b. $\overline{X}$ = 90 for a sample of n = 25
    c. $\overline{X}$ = 102 for a sample of n = 4
    d. $\overline{X}$ = 102 for a sample of n = 100

6.   The Central Limit Theorem states that the
distribution of sample means approaches a normal shape as
n approaches infinity. In more practical terms, identify
the two criteria that determine when the distribution of
sample means will form an almost perfectly normal
distribution.

7.   Because the distribution of sample means tends to
have a normal shape, we can use z-scores and the unit
normal table to find the probability of obtaining
specific samples from a given population. Remember,
whenever you are computing probabilities for sample means
you must use the distribution of sample means and the
standard error. Find each of the probabilities requested
below.

    a.   For a normal population with μ = 70 and σ = 9,
what is the probability of obtaining a sample mean
greater than 73 for a sample of n = 36 scores?

    b.   Given a normal population with μ = 40 and σ = 4,
what is the probability of obtaining a sample mean
between 39 and 41 for a sample of n = 16 scores?

    c.   A normal population has μ = 60 and σ = 10. If
you randomly select four scores from this population,

what is the probability that the scores will total more than 250? (Hint: To total 250 or more, the four scores must average at last 62.5.)

ANSWERS TO PROBLEMS

1.   The items or "scores" in a sampling distribution are statistics. If you obtain all the possible random samples for a specified sample size (n) and compute a statistic (for example the mean) for each sample, then the set of statistics is a sampling distribution.

2.   The mean of the distribution of sample means is called the expected value of $\overline{X}$ and is equal to the population mean μ . The standard deviation of the distribution of sample means is called the standard error of $\overline{X}$ and is computed by,

$$\sigma_{\overline{X}} = \frac{\sigma}{\sqrt{n}}$$

The distribution of sample means tends toward a normal shape as the sample size (n) approaches infinity.

3.   a.   The expected value is 80 and the standard error is 10/5 = 2.

      b.   The expected value is 80: and the standard error is 10/2 = 5.

c.   The population standard deviation must be 9.

4.   Standard error is the standard deviation of the distribution of sample means. Standard error measures the standard distance between $\overline{X}$ and μ .

5.   a.   The standard error is 5, and z = -2.00.
     b.   The standard error is 2, and z = -5.00.
     c.   The standard error is 5, and z = +0.40.
     d.   The standard error is 1, and z = +2.00.

6.   For practical purposes, the distribution of sample
means is nearly normal if the population is normal or if
the sample size is at least n = 30.

7.   a.   The standard error is 1.5. $P(\bar{X} > 73) = P(z >$
+2.00) = 0.0228.
     b.   The standard error is 1.   The probability is p =
.3413 + .3413 = 0.6426.
     c.   With n = 4, the standard error is 5.
$P(\bar{X} > 62.5) = P(z > +0.50) = 0.3085.$

CHAPTER **8** INTRODUCTION TO HYPOTHESIS TESTING

LEARNING OBJECTIVES

1. Understand the logic of hypothesis testing.

2. Be able to state hypotheses and find the critical region.

3. Be able to assess sample data with a z-score and make a statistical decision about the hypotheses.

4. Know the difference between Type I and Type II errors.

5.   Know how to perform hypothesis tests using the normal approximation to the binomial distribution.

NEW TERMS AND CONCEPTS

The following terms were introduced in this chapter. Define or describe each term and, where appropriate, describe how each term is related to other terms in the list.

hypothesis testing
null hypothesis
alternative hypothesis
Type I error
Type II error
alpha
level of significance
critical region
test statistic
beta
binomial test

NEW FORMULAS

$P(\text{Type I Error}) = \alpha$

$P(\text{Type II Error}) = \beta$

STEP-BY-STEP

Using a Sample to Test a Hypothesis about a Population Mean: Although the hypothesis testing procedure is presented repeatedly in the textbook, we will demonstrate one more example here. As always, we will use the standard four-step procedure. The following generic example will be used for this demonstration.

The researcher begins with a known population, in this case a normal distribution with $\mu = 50$ and $\sigma = 10$. The researcher suspects that a particular treatment will produce a change in the scores for the individuals in the population. Because it is impossible to administer the treatment to the entire population, a sample of $n = 25$ individuals is selected and the treatment is given to this sample. After receiving the treatment, the average score for this sample is $\overline{X} = 53$. Although the experiment involves only a sample, the researcher would like to use the data to make a general conclusion about how the treatment affects the entire population.

Step 1: The first step is to state the hypotheses and select an alpha level. The hypotheses always concern an unknown population. For this example, the researcher does not know what would happen if the entire population were given the treatment. Nonetheless, it is possible to make hypotheses about the effect of the treatment. Specifically, the null hypothesis says that the treatment has no effect. According to H_0, the unknown population (after treatment) is identical to the original population (before treatment). In symbols,

H_0: $\mu = 50$ (After treatment, the mean is still 50)

The alternative to the null hypothesis is that the treatment does have an effect that causes a change in the population mean. In symbols,

H_1: $\mu \neq 50$ (After treatment, the mean is different from 50)

At this time you also select the alpha-level. Traditionally, α is set at .05 or .01. If there is particular concern about a Type I Error, or if a researcher desires to present overwhelming evidence for a treatment effect, a smaller alpha-level can be used (such as α = .001).

Step 2:   The next step is to locate the critical region. You should recall that the critical region is defined as the set of outcomes that are very unlikely to be obtained if the null hypothesis is true. We begin by looking at all the possible outcomes that could be obtained, then use the alpha level to determine the outcomes that are very unlikely. For this example, we look at the distribution of sample means for n = 25; that is, all the possible sample means that could be obtained if H_0 were true.

        The distribution of sample means will be normal because the original population is normal. The expected value is μ = 50 (if H_0 is true), and the standard error for n = 25 is

$$\sigma_{\bar{x}} = \frac{\sigma}{\sqrt{n}} = \frac{10}{\sqrt{25}} = 2$$

With α = .05, we want to identify the most unlikely 5% of this distribution. The boundaries for the extreme 5% are determined by z-scores of z = $\pm$1.96.

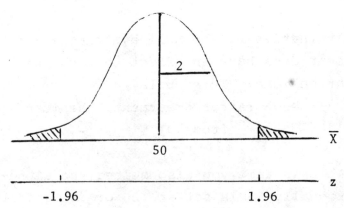

Step 3:   Obtain the Sample Data and Compute the Test
Statistic.   For this example we obtained the sample mean
of $\overline{X}$ = 53. This sample mean corresponds to a z-score
of,

$$z = \frac{\overline{X} - \mu}{\sigma_{\overline{X}}} = \frac{53 - 50}{2} = 1.50$$

Step 4:   Make Your Decision.   The z-score we obtained
is not in the critical region. This means that our
sample mean, $\overline{X}$ = 53, is not an extreme or unusual value
to be obtained from a population with μ = 50.   Therefore,
we conclude that this sample does not provide sufficient
evidence to conclude that the null hypothesis is wrong.
Our statistical decision is to fail to reject H_0. The
conclusion for the experiment is that the data do not
indicate that the treatment has a significant effect.
        Note that the decision always consists of two parts:
1) a statistical decision about the null hypothesis, and
2) a conclusion about the outcome of the experiment.

HINTS AND CAUTIONS

1.   When using samples with n > 1, we compute a z-score
for the sample mean to determine if the sample data are
unlikely. Be sure to use $\sigma_{\overline{X}}$ in the denominator,
because the z-score is locating the sample mean within
the distribution of sample means.

SELF-TEST AND REVIEW

1.   Hypothesis testing is the most commonly used

technique in inferential statistics. In general terms, this technique uses the data from a sample to draw general conclusions about an unknown population. In this chapter we introduced the procedure for testing hypotheses about a population mean. Identify and describe the two hypotheses that are evaluated in this procedure.

2.   Throughout the book we will use the same four-step procedure for hypotheses testing. Identify the four steps.

3.   Although a hypothesis test evaluates two hypotheses, the conclusion from the test always is stated in terms of the null hypothesis. We either "Reject H_0" or "Fail to Reject H_0". Explain why the statistical conclusion focuses on the null hypothesis.

4.   Because the limited data from a sample cannot provide complete information about a population, hypothesis testing is based on probabilities. The procedure is structured to avoid making a serious error, but there always is some probability that a hypothesis test will lead to the wrong conclusion.
     a.   Define a Type I Error.
     b.   Describe the consequences of a Type I Error.
     c.   What determines the probability of a Type I Error.
     d.   Define a Type II Error.
     e.   Describe the consequences of a Type II Error.

5.   The final decision in hypothesis testing is based on a comparison of the data with the null hypothesis. If the data are very different from the hypothesis, we

conclude that the hypothesis must be wrong. Otherwise, we conclude that the data do not provide sufficient evidence to reject H_0. The hypothesis testing procedure establishes criteria for making this decision by determining the boundaries for the critical region.

    a. In words, define the critical region.

    b. How is the critical region related to the alpha level?

6.   Using words, rewrite the z-score formula to show what it does conceptually in hypothesis testing. What does the standard error measure in this formula?

7.   Reaction times for a specific task are normally distributed with $\mu = 250$ and $\sigma = 50$. A particular sample of n = 25 subjects had a mean reaction time of $\overline{X} = 274$ milliseconds. Many of the subjects later complained about distracting noises during the test session.

    a. To assess whether their complaints are valid, determine if the sample data are significantly different from what would be expected. Use an alpha level of .05.

    b. Would you have reached the same conclusion if alpha had been set at .01?

8.   Scores for a standardized reading test are normally distributed with $\mu = 50$ and $\sigma = 6$ for sixth graders. A teacher suspects that his class is well above average for sixth grade and might need more challenging material. The class is given the standardized test, and the mean for the class of n = 16 students is $\overline{X} = 54.5$. Are these students significantly different from the typical sixth graders? Test with alpha set at .05.

9.   In a binomial situation where the population values
for p and q are not known, sample data can be used to
test hypotheses about these probability values. The null
hypothesis specifies values for p and q, and the critical
region is located using the normal approximation to the
binomial distribution. Suppose it is known that for a
particular breed of dog two out of ten develop hip
deformities during the first year. A certain breeder
claims to have reduced this hip problem through selective
breeding. In a sample of n = 100 dogs from this breeder
only 10 develop deformities during the first year. Does
this sample indicate that the breeder's dogs are
significantly different from the general population?
Test with α = .05.

ANSWERS TO SELF-TEST

1.   The two hypotheses are the null hypothesis (H_0) and
the alternative hypothesis (H_1). The null hypothesis
states that the treatment has no effect (no change, no
difference), and it identifies a specific value for the
unknown population mean. The alternative hypothesis
states that the treatment does have an effect and the
population mean is changed.

2.   1) State the hypotheses and select an alpha level.
      2) Locate the critical region.
      3) Obtain the data and compute the test statistic.
      4) Make your decision.

3.   Inferential reasoning involves using limited
information to make general conclusions. In hypothesis
testing we use sample data to test a hypothesis about a

population. With an inferential procedure it is impossible to prove that a general conclusion is true. However, it is possible to demonstrate that a general conclusion is false or (at least) unlikely. Therefore, the null hypothesis states that the treatment has no effect, and we hope to show that this hypothesis is false or unlikely.

4.   a. A Type I error is rejecting a true null hypothesis.

b. With a Type I error a researcher concludes that a treatment has an effect when in fact it does not. This can lead to a false report.

c. The probability of a Type I error is the alpha level selected by the researcher.

d. A Type II error is failing to reject a false null hypothesis.

d. With a Type II error a researcher concludes that the data do not provide a convincing demonstration that the treatment has any effect. The researcher may choose to refine and repeat the experiment.

5.   a. The critical region consists of experimental outcomes that would be very unlikely if the null hypothesis is true.

b. The alpha level is the probability value that is used to define "very unlikely" outcomes. With $\alpha = .05$, for example, the critical region consists of outcomes that are less than 5% likely to be obtained if the null hypothesis is true.

6. $z = \dfrac{\text{Sample Data} - \text{Population Hypothesis}}{\text{Standard Error}}$

The standard error measures the standard distance due to chance between a sample mean (data) and the population mean.

7.   a.   The critical region consists of values greater than $z = +1.96$ or less than $z = -1.96$. For this sample $z = 2.40$. Reject the null hypothesis and conclude that the data for this sample are significantly different from what would be expected by chance.
       b.   With $\alpha = .01$, the critical region consists of values greater than $z = +2.58$ or less than -2.58. By this standard, the obtained z-score is not in the critical region, so we fail to reject H_0.

8.   The null hypothesis states that these children are no different from the general population with $\mu = 50$. In symbols, $H_0: \mu = 50$. The critical region consists of z-scores beyond 1.96 or -1.96. The data produce a z-score of $z = 3.00$. Reject H_0 and conclude that this sample comes from a population with a mean that is different from $\mu = 50$.

9.   The null hypothesis states that the dogs from this breeder are not different from the general population, $H_0: p = .20$ and $q = .80$. The critical values are $z = \pm 1.96$. With $n = 100$ and $p = .20$, the binomial distribution is approximately normal with $\mu = 20$ and $\sigma = 4$. The sample value $X = 10$ corresponds to a z-score of $z = -2.50$. Reject H_0 and conclude that this breeder's dogs are significantly different.

LEARNING OBJECTIVES

1.   When an experiment contains a prediction about the
direction of a treatment effect, you should be able to
incorporate the directional prediction into the
hypothesis testing procedure and conduct a directional
(one-tailed) hypothesis test.

2.   You should be able to use sample data to make a
point estimate or an interval estimate of an unknown
population mean.

3.   You should know what information is needed to
compute the power of a statistical test and, given that
information, you should be able to compute power.

4.   You should know what factors influence the power of
a statistical test and be able to describe exactly how
each factor affects power.

NEW TERMS AND CONCEPTS

    The following terms were introduced in this chapter.
Define or describe each term and, where appropriate, describe
how each term is related to other terms in the list.

    directional test (one-tailed test)
    estimation
    point estimate
    interval estimate (confidence interval)
    power

NEW FORMULAS

$$\mu = \bar{X} \pm z \sigma_{\bar{X}}$$

$$\text{Power} = 1 - \beta$$

STEP-BY-STEP

    The following example will be used to demonstrate the
step-by-step procedures for directional hypotheses tests,
estimation, and power.
    A researcher begins with a normal population with $\mu = 60$
and $\sigma = 8$. The researcher is evaluating a specific treatment
that is expected to increase scores. The treatment is
administered to a sample of $n = 16$ individuals, and the mean
for the treated sample is $\bar{X} = 66$.

Directional Hypothesis Test: A directional hypothesis test follows the same four-step procedure that is used for all hypothesis tests.

Step 1: State the hypotheses and select an alpha level. With a directional test it is easier to begin with the alternative hypothesis because H_1 simply reflects the researcher's prediction. For this example,

H_1: $\mu > 60$ (the treatment will increase the mean)
The null hypothesis says that the treatment does not have any effect.

H_0: $\mu \leq 60$ (no increase)
For this example we will set $\alpha = .05$.

Step 2: Locate the critical region. Begin by sketching the distribution of sample means for n = 16 that would be obtained if H_0 were true. The critical region consists of sample means that tend to refute H_0 and support H_1. For this example, H_1 states that the treated population will have a mean greater than 60 so the critical region will consist of sample means greater than 60. This is the right-hand tail of the distribution. With $\alpha = .05$, a z-score of z = +1.65 forms the boundary for the critical region.

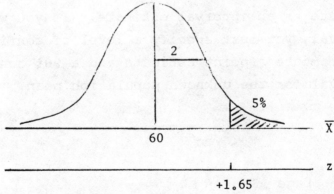

Step 3:   Obtain the data and compute the test statistic.
Our sample mean $\overline{X} = 66$ corresponds to a z-score of

$$z = \frac{\overline{X} - \mu}{\sigma_{\overline{X}}} = \frac{66 - 60}{2} = 3.00$$

Step 4:   Make Decision.   The z-score we obtained is in
the critical region.   The statistical decision is to
reject H_o.   On the basis of these data, the researcher
can conclude that the treatment produces a significant
increase in the population mean.

Estimation: For our example, the researcher does not know
the mean for the population after treatment.   The researcher
expects that the treated population will have a mean greater
than 60 because the treatment is expected to increase scores.
However, the only available information comes from the sample
mean which can be used to estimate the mean for the unknown
population.

Step 1:   Begin with the basic formula for estimation.
Remember, this is simply the regular z-score formula that
has been solved for μ.

$$\mu = \overline{X} \pm z\sigma_{\overline{X}}$$

Step 2:   Determine whether you are computing a point
estimate or an interval estimate.   If you want an
interval, you must specify a level of confidence.   We
will compute a point estimate and a 90% confidence
interval for the unknown population mean.

Chapter 9 -   page 98

Step 3:   Find the appropriate z-score values to
substitute in the equation. For a point estimate, always
use z = 0 which is the point in the exact middle of the
distribution. For a 90% confidence interval, we want the
z-score values that form the boundaries for the middle
90% of the distribution. These values are obtained from
the unit normal table. You should find that 90% of a
normal distribution is contained between z = +1.65 and
z = -1.65.

Step 4:   Compute $\bar{X}$ and $\sigma_{\bar{X}}$ from the sample data. For
this example we are given $\bar{X}$ = 66 and you can compute

$$\sigma_{\bar{X}} = \frac{\sigma}{\sqrt{n}} = \frac{8}{\sqrt{16}} = \frac{8}{4} = 2$$

Step 5:   Substitute the appropriate values in the
estimation equation.

point estimate   interval estimate

μ =   66 $\pm$ 0 μ =   66 $\pm$ (1.65)(2)
  = 66   = 66 $\pm$ 3.30

                                        Estimate between
                                        62.70 and 69.30

Power: Power is defined as the probability of rejecting a
false null hypothesis. To compute power you must have a
specific hypothesis test (including the null hypothesis, alpha
level, and sample size) and you must have a specific
alternative hypothesis. Often the alternative hypothesis is
specified in terms of the magnitude of the treatment effect.
For this example H_o states that the population mean after
treatment is still μ = 60. We will use a two-tailed

hypothesis test with α = .05. We will compute power for the hypothesis test assuming that the treatment has a 7-point effect. That is, we assume that the treatment increases the mean to μ = 67.

Step 1:   Locate the critical region as if you were doing a regular hypothesis test. For this example, sketch the distribution of sample means that would be expected if H_o were true and identify the boundaries for the extreme 5% of the distribution. Draw a long vertical line to indicate each critical boundary and clearly label the critical region as the area where we will reject H_o. We will identify this distribution as the Null Distribution.

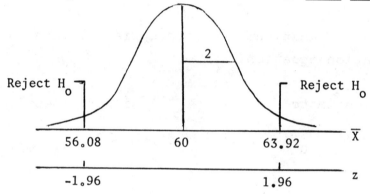

Step 2:   Still working with the null distribution, find the sample mean values that correspond to the z-score boundaries for the critical region. In our null distribution we have μ = 60 and $\sigma_{\overline{X}}$ = 2. With these parameters, a z-score of +1.96 corresponds to

$\overline{X} = \mu + z\,\sigma_{\overline{X}}$

= 60 + (1.96)(2)

= 60 + 3.92

= 63.92

The z-score of -1.96 corresponds to

$$\bar{X} = \mu + z \, \sigma_{\bar{X}}$$
$$= 60 + (-1.96)(2)$$
$$= 60 - 3.92$$
$$= 56.08$$

Write in these $\bar{X}$ values on your sketch of the null distribution.

Step 3:   Sketch the alternative distribution beside your drawing of the null distribution.   To do this you first locate the position of the alternative mean; in this case μ = 67.   Then draw another normal distribution centered at this mean.   Remember, the two distributions have the same standard error.   This second distribution is called the Alternative Distribution and it shows the set of all possible sample means that could be obtained if H_1 were true.

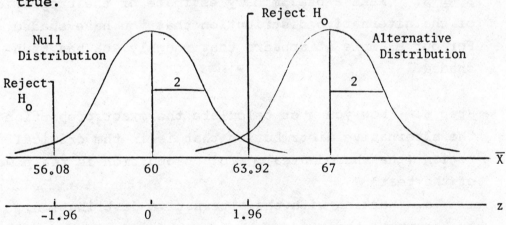

Step 4: Look at the alternative distribution and shade in the portion of this distribution that is located in the critical region. Usually you can ignore one tail of the critical region because it has essentially no overlap with the alternative distribution.

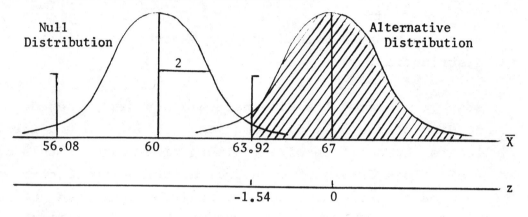

Step 5: Make a preliminary estimate of the proportion of the alternative distribution that you have shaded. For our example it appears that roughly 90% has been shaded.

Step 6: Now you must calculate the exact proportion of the alternative distribution that is in the critical region (the shaded area). This proportion is the power of the test.

    a. Working with the alternative distribution, compute the z-score that corresponds to the critical boundary. In our alternative distribution $\mu = 67$ and $\sigma_{\overline{X}} = 2$, so the boundary $\overline{X} = 63.92$ corresponds to

$$z = \frac{\overline{X} - \mu}{\sigma_{\overline{X}}} = \frac{63.92 - 67}{2} = -1.54$$

b. Look up this z-score in the unit normal table to determine the proportion. From column B of the table, .4382 of the distribution is located between and z = -1.54. The total area we have shaded is .4382 + .5000 = .9382. This is the power of the statistical test.

Step 7: Compare your final answer with the preliminary estimate you made in Step 5. If these two answers are not in agreement, check your calculations.

HINTS AND CAUTIONS

1. When computing a confidence interval after a hypothesis test, many students incorrectly take the z-score value that was computed in the hypothesis test and use this value in the estimation equation. Remember, the z-score in the estimation equation is determined by the level of confidence and the unit normal table. For example, an 80% confidence interval always uses z = ±1.28 no matter what z-score was obtained from the hypothesis test.

2. When stating the hypotheses for a directional test, remember that the predicted outcome (an increase or a decrease in μ) is stated in the alternative hypothesis (H_1).

3. To compute power for a statistical test you must begin with a specific null hypothesis and a specific alternative hypothesis which is determined by the magnitude of the treatment effect. For example, if H_o states that $\mu = 50$ and you expect the treatment to add 20

points, then the specific alternative hypothesis would state that $\mu = 70$. These two hypotheses produce two different distributions, a "null" distribution and an "alternative" distribution. The null distribution is drawn first and the critical region is located just as if you were doing a hypothesis test. Then the alternative distribution is drawn and the power of the test is determined by the proportion of the alternative distribution that is located in the critical region.

SELF TEST AND REVIEW

1. When a researcher has a specific prediction about the direction of a treatment effect (increase or decrease), it is possible to use a directional, or one-tailed, hypothesis test. Explain why this type of test is called "one-tailed."

2. When stating the hypotheses for a directional test remember H_1 says that the treatment will be effective, and H_o says that the treatment will have no effect. Suppose that a researcher is evaluating the effect of a treatment on a population where the mean is known to be $\mu = 50$.

   a. If the researcher expects the treatment to produce an increase in scores, state the null hypothesis and the alternative hypothesis for a directional test.

   b. State the directional hypothesis if the researcher is predicting that the treatment will cause a decrease in scores.

3.   For a directional hypothesis test with z-scores the
critical region is located entirely in one tail of the
distribution. To determine which tail of the
distribution will be the critical region, remember that
the critical region is defined as the set of outcomes
that tend to refute the null hypothesis. Equivalently,
you can think of the critical region as the set of
outcomes that tend to support the alternative hypothesis
(i.e., the outcomes that support the researcher's
prediction).

    a. If a researcher is predicting that a treatment
    will increase scores, which tail (right-hand or
    left-hand) will contain the critical region for a
    directional test?

    b. Where would the critical region be located if
    the researcher is predicting that the treatment will
    decrease scores?

4.   Explain why many researchers consider one-tailed
tests inappropriate for evaluating experimental results.

5.   Each year the state college accepts a group of
marginally qualified students who are designated as
"special admits." In the past these students have
finished their first year with a mean grade point average
of $\mu = 2.01$ with $\sigma = 0.40$. Last summer the college
conducted a special summer program to help prepare
special admit students for their freshman year. The
sample of $n = 25$ students in the special program
completed the year with a mean grade point average of $\bar{X} =$
2.19. On the basis of these data can the college
conclude that the summer program produces a significant
increase in performance for special admit students? Use
a one-tailed test with $\alpha = .05$.

6.   The process of using sample data to estimate population parameters is known as estimation. In this chapter we examined the process of using a sample mean as the basis for estimating an unknown population mean. The population mean can be estimated using either a point estimate or an interval estimate.

   a.   Define these two types of estimation.
   b.   Describe point estimates and interval estimates in terms of confidence and precision.

7.   Estimation often is used after a hypothesis test. Although these two inferential techniques involve many of the same calculations, they are intended to answer different questions. In general terms, what information is provided by a hypothesis test and what information is provided by estimation?

8.   The procedures for estimating μ are based on the fact that a sample mean, on average, provides an accurate, unbiased estimate of its population mean. Thus, $\bar{X}$ is always used as the point estimate of μ, and $\bar{X}$ always forms the midpoint of a confidence interval for μ. The width of a confidence interval is influenced by other factors.

   a.   Explain how the width of a confidence interval is related to the sample size, n.
   b.   Explain how the width of a confidence interval is related to the level of confidence (the % confidence).

9.   A sample of n = 16 scores is obtained from a normal population with $\sigma = 12$. The sample mean is $\bar{X} = 43$.

   a.   Use these data to make a point estimate of the population mean.

b. Make an interval estimate of μ so that you are 90% confident that the mean is in your interval.

10. Power is defined as the probability that a hypothesis test will reject a false null hypothesis. Power is not a single value but depends on the magnitude of the treatment effect. Explain how power is related to the size of the treatment effect.

11. The concept of power is closely related to the probability of a Type II Error. Identify the symbols that are used to identify power and the probability of a Type II error.

12. When planning an experiment a researcher can control several factors that will influence power.
    a. What is the effect on power of increasing sample size?
    b. How does the choice of a one-tailed versus a two-tailed test affect power?
    c. How is power related to the alpha-level of a hypothesis test?

13. A researcher studying animal learning is investigating the effectiveness of a new training procedure. Under regular circumstances, rats require an average of $\mu = 35$ errors with $\sigma = 10$ before they master a standard problem-solving task. The researcher expects that the new procedure will reduce errors by an average of five. If the researcher tests the effectiveness of the new procedure using a sample of n = 25 rats, what is the power of the hypothesis test assuming that the treatment produces a 5-point reduction in errors. Use a two-tailed test with $\alpha = .05$.

ANSWERS TO SELF-TEST

1. A directional hypothesis test often is called a one-tailed test because the entire critical region is located in one tail of the distribution.

2. a. H_0: $\mu \leq 50$ (no increase)
        H_1: $\mu > 50$ (increase)

    b. H_0: $\mu \geq 50$ (no decrease)
        H_1: $\mu < 50$ (decrease)

3. a. The critical region consists of data that are very unlikely if the null hypothesis is true. Equivalently, the critical region consists of data that are likely to be obtained if the treatment works. When a researcher is predicting an increase in scores, the critical region will be in the right-hand tail.
    b. When a researcher is predicting a decrease in scores, the critical region will be in the left-hand tail.

4. To reject the null hypothesis, a researcher must demonstrate that the data are very different from the hypothesis. With a one-tailed test, a relatively small difference is sufficient to reject H_0. For this reason, many researchers believe that one-tailed tests make it too easy to reject H_0.

5.   The college is expecting an increase, so the
hypotheses would be

H_O: $\mu \leq 2.01$ (no increase)
H_1: $\mu > 2.01$ (increase)

The critical region consists of z-scores greater than
+1.65.   For these data, z = 2.25.   Reject the null
hypothesis and conclude that the students in the special
program scored significantly higher than the general
population of special admit students.

6.   a.   For a point estimate, a single value is used to
estimate the population mean.   For an interval estimate,
the population mean is estimated to be contained within a
range of values.
     b.   Point estimates have great precision but not
confidence.   Interval estimates have increased confidence
but less precision.

7.   A hypothesis test is intended to determine whether
or not a treatment effect exists.   Estimation is used to
determine how much effect.

8.   a.   As the sample size increases, the standard error
decreases and the width of the confidence interval
decreases.
     b.   As the level of confidence increases the width
of the confidence interval also increases.

9.   a.   Use $\bar{X} = 43$ as the point estimate of μ.
     b.   The 90% confidence interval extends from 38.05
to 47.95.

10.   Power is the probability that a hypothesis test will correctly detect a treatment effect.   The larger the treatment effect, the more likely it is to be detected. Therefore, power increases as the size of the treatment effect increases.

11.   The probability of a Type II error is β and power is $1 - \beta$.

12.   a.   Increasing sample size gives the researcher more information about the population.   This means that it is more likely that the researcher will uncover a treatment effect if one exists.   Thus, increasing sample size will increase power.
     b.   A one-tailed test makes it easier to reject the null hypothesis, which will increase the power of the test.
     c.   The larger the alpha level, the easier it is to reject the null hypothesis.   Thus, the larger the alpha, the greater the power of the test.

13.   For this test, a sample mean less than $\bar{X} = 31.08$ would be in the critical region.   If the new procedure reduces the population mean to $\mu = 30$, the probability of obtaining a sample mean less than 31.08 would be $p = 0.7054$.   This is the power of the researcher's test.

CHAPTER 10 INTRODUCTION TO THE T STATISTIC

LEARNING OBJECTIVES

1.   Know when you must use the t statistic rather than a z-score for hypothesis testing.

2.   Understand the concept of degrees of freedom and how it relates to the t distribution.

3.   Be able to perform all of the necessary computations for hypothesis tests and estimation with the t statistic.

NEW TERMS AND CONCEPTS

The following terms were introduced in this chapter. Define or describe each term and, where appropriate, describe how each term is related to other terms in the list.

> t statistic
> estimated standard error
> degrees of freedom
> t distribution

NEW FORMULAS

$$s_{\bar{X}} = \frac{s}{\sqrt{n}}$$

$$t = \frac{\bar{X} - \mu}{s_{\bar{X}}}$$

$$df = n - 1$$

$$\mu = \bar{X} \pm t s_{\bar{X}}$$

STEP-BY-STEP

Hypothesis Testing with the t Statistic: The t statistic presented in this chapter is used to test a hypothesis about an unknown population mean using the data from a single sample. Calculation of the t statistic requires the sample mean $\bar{X}$ and some measure of the sample variability (either SS, s, or s^2). A hypothesis test with the t statistic uses the same four-step procedure that we use for all hypothesis tests. However, with a t statistic, you must compute the standard deviation for the sample of scores and you must remember to use the t distribution table to locate the critical values for the test. We will use the following example to demonstrate the t statistic hypothesis test.

A psychologist has prepared an "Optimism Test" that is administered yearly to graduating college seniors. The test measures how each graduating class feels about its future -- the higher the score, the more optimistic the class. Last year's class had a mean score of μ = 56. A sample of n = 25 seniors from this year's class produced an average score of $\overline{X}$ = 59 with SS = 2400. On the basis of this sample can the psychologist conclude that this year's class has a different level of optimism than last year's class? Test at the .05 level of significance.

Note that this test will use a t statistic because the population standard deviation is not known.

Step 1:   State Hypotheses and select an alpha level. The statements of the null hypothesis and the alternative hypothesis are the same for the t statistic test as they were for the z-score test.

H_o: μ = 56   (no change)

H_1: $\mu \neq 56$ (this year's mean is different)

For this example we are using α = .05

Step 2: Locate the critical region. With a sample of n = 25, the t statistic will have df = 24.   For a two-tailed test with α = .05 and df = 24, the critical t values are t = $\pm$2.064.

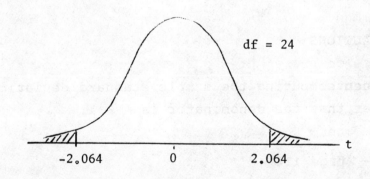

Step 3: Obtain the data and compute the test statistic: For this sample we have $\bar{X} = 59$, SS = 2400, and n = 25. To compute the t statistic for these data, it is best to start by calculating the sample standard deviation.

$$ s = \sqrt{\frac{SS}{n-1}} = \sqrt{\frac{2400}{24}} = \sqrt{100} = 10 $$

Next, use the sample standard deviation to compute the estimated standard error. Remember, standard error provides a measure of the standard distance between a sample mean $\bar{X}$ and its population mean μ.

$$ s_{\bar{X}} = \frac{s}{\sqrt{n}} = \frac{10}{\sqrt{25}} = 2 $$

Finally, compute the t statistic using the hypothesized value of μ from H_o.

$$ t = \frac{\bar{X} - \mu}{s_{\bar{X}}} = \frac{59 - 56}{2} = 1.50 $$

Step 4: Make decision. The t statistic we obtained is not in the critical region. Because there is nothing unusual about this t statistic (it is the kind of value that is likely to be obtained by chance), we fail to reject H_o. These data do not provide sufficient evidence to conclude that this year's graduating class has a level of optimism that is different from last year's class.

HINTS AND CAUTIONS

1.   When computing the sample standard deviation, remember that the denominator is n - 1.

2.   A common source of confusion occurs in the computation of the estimated standard error, $s_{\bar{x}}$. Remember, the correct denominator is $\sqrt{n}$, just as it is for $\sigma_{\bar{x}}$.   Often students are tempted to n - 1 in the denominator.

3.   When locating the critical region for a t test, be sure to consult the t distribution table, not the unit normal table.

SELF-TEST AND REVIEW

1.   In circumstances where the population standard deviation is not known, you cannot compute the standard error $\sigma_{\bar{x}}$, and you cannot compute a z-score to be used for either a hypothesis test or for estimation. In these circumstances, a t statistic is used in place of a z-score. Explain how the t statistic avoids the problem of an unknown population standard deviation.

2.   Standard error is used in the z-score formula to provide an estimate of how much distance is expected, on average, between a sample mean $\bar{X}$ and its population mean μ. In the formula for the t statistic, the standard error is replaced by the estimated standard error.
      a.   A sample of n = 25 scores is selected from a population with σ = 20. What is the standard error for this sample?
      b.   A sample of n = 25 scores has a sample standard deviation of s = 20. What is the estimated standard error for this sample?

3.   The basis of the t statistic involves using the
sample data to compute the sample standard deviation, s,
to be used in place of the unknown population standard
deviation σ.
       a.   Compute the sample standard deviation for the
following set of scores.
       b.   Use the sample standard deviation to compute the
estimated standard error, $s_{\bar{X}}$, for this sample.
             Scores: 5, 1, 10, 3, 8, 3, 2, 7, 6

4.   Each t statistic has an associated value for degrees
of freedom, df.   There is a family of t distributions,
and the exact shape of any particular distribution
depends on the value of df.
       a.   A t statistic computed for a sample of n = 10
scores would have df = _____.
       b.   Find the critical values of t for a two-tailed
hypothesis test with α = .05, using a sample of n = 25
scores.
       c.   Find the critical value of t for a one-tailed
hypothesis test with α = .05, using a sample of n = 30
scores.

5.   The t statistic also can be used to make point
estimates or interval estimates of the population mean.
The t statistic formula is solved for μ to obtain the
estimation formula.
$$\mu = \bar{X} \pm ts_{\bar{X}}$$

The values of $\bar{X}$ and $s_{\bar{X}}$ are computed entirely from the
sample data.
       a.   For a point estimate of μ, what value is used
for t in the estimation equation?
       b.   For an 80% confidence interval based on a sample

of n = 9 scores, what values of t would be used to compute the two ends of the confidence interval?

    c. For a specific sample, if the level of confidence is increased, what happens to the width of the confidence interval?

    d. In general, if sample size (n) is increased, what happens to the width of the confidence interval?

6. A company embarks on a new program to boost morale and reduce the amount of absenteeism. The president of the company sets a goal of $\mu = 7$ absences per year for the employees. The personnel director believes this goal is overly optimistic and cannot be achieved. One year after the program's enactment, the director obtained a random sample of n = 16 employees and found an average of $\bar{X} = 9.5$ absences with s = 4.

    a. Do the sample data support the director's view? Is there a significant difference between the sample data and the president's goal? Test with $\alpha = .05$.

    b. What statistical decision would have been made if α were set at .01?

    c. Estimate the mean number of absences for the entire population (μ) using a 90% confidence interval.

7. Upon enrolling in State University, freshmen are required to take an English placement exam. Over the past few years, students have averaged $\mu = 46$. A professor noted that students from a particular high school seemed to perform better on the exam. A sample of n = 9 of these students showed an average score of $\bar{X} = 49$ and SS = 648.

    a. Do these data suggest that the students who attend that particular high school are better prepared? Use a one-tailed test with $\alpha = .05$.

b.   Use the sample data to estimate μ for students who attend the high school in question. Make a point estimate and an interval estimate at the 80% level of confidence.

8.   Public employees for State A are paid on the average μ = 12.5 dollars per hour. Just over the border in State B, summary statistics of average wages are not made available. However, a random sample of n = 4 public employees from State B showed the following hourly wages:
       $8, $8, $16, $8
       a.   Is the pay for workers in State B significantly different from the pay for workers in State A? Test at the .05 level.
       b.   Estimate the average wage, μ, for the population of workers in State B. Make a point estimate and an interval estimate at the 90% level of confidence.

ANSWERS TO SELF-TEST

1.   The t statistic uses the sample standard deviation (s) to estimate the unknown population standard deviation (σ).

2.   a.   The standard error is $\sigma_{\bar{x}}$ = 20/5 = 4.
     b.   The estimated standard error is $s_{\bar{x}}$ = 20/5 = 4

3.   a.   For these data, SS = 72, the sample variance is 9, and the sample standard deviation is s = 3.
     b. $s_{\bar{x}}$ = 3/3 = 1.

4.   a.   df = n - 1 = 9
      b.   t = $\pm$2.064
      c.   t = 1.699

5.   a.   Always use t = 0 for a point estimate.
      b.   t = $\pm$1.397
      c.   If the level of confidence is increased, the
interval will be wider.
      d.   If the sample size is increased, the interval
will be narrower.

6.   a.   The null hypothesis states that employee
absences are not different from the president's goal, H_o: μ
= 7.   WIth df = 15, the critical region boundaries are t
= $\pm$2.131.   For these data, t = 2.5.   Reject H_o and
conclude that the employees are different from the
president's goal.
      b.   With α = .01, the critical region boundaries are
t = $\pm$2.947.   By this standard the data are not in the
critical region and you would fail to reject H_o.
      c.   For 90% confidence, use t = +_ 1.753.   The
interval extends from 11.253 to 7.747 absences.

7.   a.   The professor suspects that these students are
better than average; that is, they come from a population
with μ > 46.   The directional hypotheses are:

      H_o: $\mu \le$ 46   (not better)
      H_1: μ > 46   (better)

With df = 8, the critical region consists of t values
greater than 1.860.   The t statistic for these data is t
= 1.00.   Fail to reject H_o.   These data do not provide
sufficient evidence to conclude that students from the

specific high school are different from the general
population.

   b.   Use the sample mean $\bar{X}$ = 49 for the point
estimate for   μ.   For 80% confidence, use t = $^\pm$1.397.
The 80% confidence interval extends from 53.191 to
44.809.   We are 80% confident that the sample comes from
a population with a mean within this range.

9.   a.   The null hypothesis says that there is no
difference between the two states.
      H_o: μ = $12.5 for State B
      H_1: μ ≠ $12.5 for State B

With df = 3, the critical values are t = $^\pm$3.182.   For
these data, SS = 48 and the t statistic is t = -1.25.
Fail to reject H_o.   The data do not show a significant
difference in wages between the two states.
   b.   For the point estimate, use $\bar{X}$ = $10.00.   For 90%
confidence, use t = ±2.353.   The 90% confidence interval
extends from 14.706 to 5.294.   We are 90% confident that
the population mean wage for State B is between $14.706
and $5.294.

CHAPTER **11**   STATISTICAL INFERENCE WITH TWO
INDEPENDENT SAMPLES

LEARNING OBJECTIVES

1.   You should be able to describe and to recognize the
experimental situations where an independent measures t
statistic is appropriate for statistical inference.

2. You should be able to use the independent measures t
statistic to test hypotheses about the mean difference
between two populations (or between two treatment
conditions).

3.   You should be able to use the independent measures t
statistic to make a point estimate or an interval
estimate of the mean difference between two populations
(or between two treatment conditions).

4. You should be able to list the assumptions that must be satisfied before an independent measures t statistic can be computed or interpreted.

NEW TERMS AND CONCEPTS

The following terms were introduced in this chapter. Define or describe each term and, where appropriate, describe how each term is related to others in the list.

independent measures design (between subjects design)
pooled variance
homogeneity of variance

NEW FORMULAS

$$t = \frac{(\overline{X}_1 - \overline{X}_2) - (\mu_1 - \mu_2)}{s_{\overline{X} - \overline{X}}} \qquad s_{\overline{X} - \overline{X}} = \sqrt{\frac{s_p^2}{n_1} + \frac{s_p^2}{n_2}}$$

$$s_p^2 = \frac{SS_1 + SS_2}{df_1 + df_2}$$

$$\mu_1 - \mu_2 = (\overline{X}_1 - \overline{X}_2) \pm t s_{\overline{X} - \overline{X}}$$

Hypothesis Tests with the Independent Measures t Statistic. The independent measures t statistic is used in situations where a researcher wants to test a hypothesis about the difference between two population means using the data from two separate (independent) samples. The test requires both sample means ($\bar{X}_1$ and $\bar{X}_2$), and some measure of the variability for each sample (usually SS). The following example will be used to demonstrate the independent measures t hypothesis test.

A researcher wants to assess the damage to memory that is caused by chronic alcoholism. A sample of n = 10 alcoholics is obtained from a hospital treatment ward, and a control group of n = 10 non-drinkers is obtained from the hospital maintenance staff. Each person is given a brief memory test and the researcher records the memory score for each subject. The data are summarized as follows:

Alcoholics	Control
$\bar{X}$ = 43	$\bar{X}$ = 57
SS = 400	SS = 410

Step 1: State the hypotheses and select an alpha level. As always, the null hypothesis states that there is no effect.

H_0: $(\mu_1 - \mu_2) = 0$ (no difference)

The alternative hypothesis says that there is a difference between the two population means.

H_1: $(\mu_1 - \mu_2) \neq 0$

We will use $\alpha = .05$.

Step 2: Locate the critical region. With n = 10 in each sample, the t statistic will have degrees of freedom equal to,

$$df = n_1 + n_2 - 2 = 18$$

Sketch the entire distribution of t statistics with df = 18 and locate the extreme 5%. The critical values are t = ±2.101.

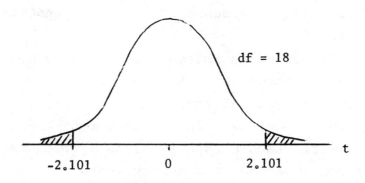

Step 3: Compute the t statistic. It is easiest to begin by computing the pooled variance for the two samples.

$$s_p^2 = \frac{SS_1 + SS_2}{df_1 + df_2} = \frac{400 + 410}{9 + 9} = \frac{810}{18} = 45$$

Next, calculate the standard error for the t statistic.

$$s_{\bar{x} - \bar{x}} = \sqrt{\frac{s_p^2}{n_1} + \frac{s_p^2}{n_2}} = \sqrt{\frac{45}{10} + \frac{45}{10}} = \sqrt{9} = 3$$

Finally, use the two sample means and the standard error to calculate the t statistic.

$$t = \frac{(\bar{X}_1 - \bar{X}_2) - (\mu_1 - \mu_2)}{s_{\bar{x} - \bar{x}}} = \frac{(43 - 57) - 0}{3} = -4.67$$

Step 4: Make decision. The t statistic for these data is in the critical region. This is a very unlikely outcome ($p < .05$) if H_o is true, therefore, we reject H_o. The researcher concludes that there is a significant difference between the mean memory score for chronic alcoholics and the mean score for non-drinkers.

HINTS AND CAUTIONS

1. One of the most common errors in computing the independent measures t statistic occurs when students confuse the formulas for pooled variance and standard error. To compute the pooled variance, you combine the two samples into a single estimated variance. The formula for pooled variance uses a single fraction with SS in the numerator and df in the denominator:

$$s_p^2 = \frac{SS_1 + SS_2}{df_1 + df_2}$$

To compute the standard error, you add the separate errors for the two samples. In the formula for standard error these two separate sources of error appear as two separate fractions:

$$s_{\bar{x} - \bar{x}} = \sqrt{\frac{s_p^2}{n_1} + \frac{s_p^2}{n_2}}$$

SELF-TEST AND REVIEW

1.   Briefly describe what is meant by an "independent measures" experiment.

2.   The independent measures t statistic uses the data from two separate samples to evaluate the difference between two population means. In symbols and in words, state the null hypothesis for the independent measures t hypothesis test.

3.   Like the single-sample t statistic, the independent measures t has degrees of freedom.
    a.   What is the formula for df for the independent measures t statistic?
    b.   If an independent measures experiment has n = 10 in one sample and n = 15 in the second sample, then the t statistic would have df = _____.
    c.   A researcher reports a t statistic with df = 20 from an independent measures experiment. How many individual subjects participated in the experiment?

4.   To compute the independent measures t statistic you first must combine the two sample variances into a single value called the pooled variance.
    a.   Find the pooled variance for the following two samples:

        Sample 1:   n = 7 and SS = 58
        Sample 2:   n = 5 and SS = 42
    b.   Find the pooled variance for the following two

samples. (Hint: When two samples are the same size, you can simply average the two variances. Otherwise, it is easier to compute SS for each sample, then use the formula for pooled variance.)

Sample 1:   n = 12 and s^2 = 4
Sample 2:   n = 10 and s^2 = 6

5.   To justify pooling the two sample variances, the data must satisfy the homogeneity of variance assumption. In symbols and in words state the homogeneity assumption.

6.   The independent measures t statistic also can be used for estimation. Specifically, the sample mean difference is used as the basis for estimating the difference between two population means. When used for estimation, the terms in the independent measures t formula are reorganized and the resulting equation is:

$$(\mu_1 - \mu_2) = \bar{X}_1 - \bar{X}_2 \pm ts_{\bar{X} - \bar{X}}$$

The difference between the sample means and the standard error are computed directly from the sample data.
    a.   For a point estimate of the difference between the population means, what value of t is used in the equation?
    b.   For an 80% confidence interval based on two samples with n = 10 in each, what t values should be used in the equation to determine the two ends of the confidence interval?

7.   A researcher would like to demonstrate how different schedules of reinforcement can influence behavior. Two separate groups of rats are trained to press a bar in

order to receive a food pellet. One group is trained
using a fixed ratio schedule where they receive one
pellet for every 10 presses of the bar. The second group
is trained using a fixed interval schedule where they
receive one pellet for the first bar press that occurs
within a 30 second interval. Note that the second group
must wait 30 seconds before another pellet is possible no
matter how many times the bar is pressed. After 4 days
of training, the researcher records the response rate
(number of presses per minute) for each rat. The results
are summarized as follows:

Fixed Ratio	Fixed Interval
n = 4	n = 8
$\bar{X}$ = 30	$\bar{X}$ = 18
SS = 90	SS = 150

a. Do these data indicate that there is a
significant difference in responding for these two
reinforcement schedules? Test at the .05 level of
significance.

b. Estimate the population mean difference in
response rates between these two reinforcement schedules.
Use a point estimate and an 80% confidence interval.

8. A psychologist is examining the educational
advantages of a preschool program. A sample of 24 fourth
grade children is obtained. Half of these children had
attended preschool and the others had not. The
psychologist records the scholastic achievement score for
each child and obtained the following data:

Preschool			No Preschool		
8	6	8	8	5	7
9	7	7	6	8	5
6	9	8	7	5	6
9	7	8	7	5	6

Do these data indicate that participation in a preschool program gives children a significant <u>advantage</u> in scholastic achievement? Use a <u>one-tailed</u> test at the .05 level.

9.   Use a F-max test to determine whether or not the data from problem 8 satisfy the homogeneity of variance assumption.

10.   The following data are from two separate samples. Does it appear that these two samples came from the same population or from two different populations?
     a.   Use an F-max test to determine whether there is evidence for a significant difference between the two population variances. Use the .05 level of significance.
     b.   Use an independent measures t test to determine whether there is evidence for a significant difference between the two population means. Again, use the .05 level of significance.

Sample 1	Sample 2
n = 10	n = 10
$\bar{X}$ = 32	$\bar{X}$ = 18
SS = 890	SS = 550

1. An independent measures experiment uses a separate, or independent, sample for each treatment condition.

2. The null hypothesis states that there is no difference between the two population means. In symbols,

$$H_o: \quad (\mu_1 - \mu_2) = 0$$

3. a. $df = (n_1 - 1) + (n_2 - 1)$
$$= n_1 + n_2 - 2$$
   b. $df = 9 + 14 = 23$
   c. There are a total of 22 subjects in the two samples.

4. a. pooled variance = $100/10 = 10$
   b. For sample 1, SS = 44. For sample 2, SS = 54. The pooled variance is $98/20 = 4.9$.

5. The homogeneity of variance assumption states that the two populations from which the samples are obtained have the same variance. In symbols, $\sigma_1^2 = \sigma_2^2$.

6. a. Always use $t = 0$ for a point estimate.
   b. With $df = 18$, the t scores are $t = +1.330$ and $t = -1.330$

7. a. With $df = 10$, the critical t values are $t = \pm 2.228$. These data have a pooled variance of 24 and produce a t statistic of $t = 4.00$. Reject H_0. The data provide sufficient evidence to conclude that there is a significant difference between the two schedules.

b. For the point estimate use $\bar{X}_1 - \bar{X}_2 = 12$ points. For an 80% confidence interval, use $t = \pm 1.372$. The interval extends from 7.884 to 16.116.

8. The psychologist expects the preschool children (sample 1) to have higher scores, so the directional hypotheses are,

$$H_0: \ (\mu_1 - \mu_2) \leq 0 \quad \text{(preschool is not higher)}$$
$$H_1: \ (\mu_1 - \mu_2) > 0 \quad \text{(preschool is higher)}$$

The critical region consists of t values greater than $t = +1.717$. For these data, $SS_1 = 12.67$ and $SS_2 = 14.25$. The pooled variance is 1.22, and $t = 3.16$. Reject H_0 and conclude that the preschool children score significantly higher on the scholastic achievement test.

9. The two sample variances are 1.15 and 1.30. F-max = 1.13. The critical value is 3.28 (using df = 12), so we fail to reject H_0. There is no significant difference between the two sample variances.

10. a. For these data, F-max = 1.62. The critical value for $\alpha = .05$ is 4.03. Fail to reject H_0. There is not sufficient evidence to conclude that the two population variances are different.

b. For these data the pooled variance is 80 and the t statistic is $t = 14/4 = 3.50$. Reject H_0 and conclude that the two population means are different.

CHAPTER 12

STATISTICAL INFERENCE WITH TWO RELATED SAMPLES

LEARNING OBJECTIVES

1.   Know the difference between independent measures and repeated measures experimental designs.

2. Be able to perform the computations for the repeated measures t test.

3.   Be able to estimate the value of μ_D using the repeated measures t statistic.

4.   Understand the advantages and disadvantages of the repeated measures design and when this type of study is appropriate.

NEW TERMS AND CONCEPTS

The following terms were introduced in this chapter.

Define or describe each term and, where appropriate, describe
how each term is related to other terms in the list.

     repeated measures design
     repeated measures t statistic
     estimated standard error of $\bar{D}$
     individual differences
     matched subjects design
     carry-over effects

NEW FORMULAS

$$\bar{D} = \frac{\Sigma D}{n}$$

$$s_{\bar{D}} = \frac{s}{\sqrt{n}}$$

$$t = \frac{\bar{D} - \mu_D}{s_{\bar{D}}}$$

$$\mu_D = \bar{D} \pm t s_{\bar{D}}$$

STEP-BY-STEP

Hypothesis Testing with the Repeated Measures t. The
repeated measures t statistic is used to test for a mean
difference (μ_D) between two treatment conditions using data
from a single sample of subjects where each individual is
measured first in one treatment condition and then in the
second condition. This test statistic also is used for
matched subjects designs which consists of two samples with
the subjects in one sample matched one-to-one with the
subjects in the second sample. Often, a repeated measures

experiment consists of a "before/after" design where each
subject is measured before treatment and then again after
treatment. The following example will be used to demonstrate
the repeated measures t test.

A researcher would like to determine whether a particular
treatment has an effect on performance scores. A sample of n
= 16 subjects is selected. Each subject is measured before
receiving the treatment and again after treatment. The
researcher records the difference between the two scores for
each subject. The difference scores averaged $\bar{D}$ = -6 with SS =
960.

Step 1: State the hypotheses and select an alpha level.
In the experiment the treatment was given to a sample,
but the researcher wants to determine whether the
treatment has any effect for the general population. As
always, the null hypothesis says that there is no effect.

H_0: μ_D = 0 (on average, the before/after difference
for the population is zero)

The alternative hypothesis states that the treatment does
produce a difference.

H_1: μ_D $\neq$ 0

We will use α = .05.

Step 2: Locate the critical region. With a sample of n
= 16 the repeated measures t statistic will have df = 15.
Sketch the distribution of t statistics with df = 15 and
locate the extreme 5% of the distribution. The critical
boundaries are t = ± 2.131.

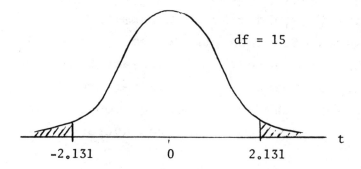

df = 15

-2.131   0   2.131   t

Step 3: Calculate the test statistic. As with all t statistics, it is easier to begin the calculation with the denominator of the t formula. For this example, the standard deviation for the difference scores is

$$s = \sqrt{\frac{SS}{n-1}} = \sqrt{\frac{960}{15}} = \sqrt{64} = 8$$

With a sample of n = 16, the standard error is

$$s_{\bar{D}} = \frac{s}{\sqrt{n}} = \frac{8}{\sqrt{16}} = \frac{8}{4} = 2$$

Finally, substitute the sample mean difference and the standard error in the t formula,

$$t = \frac{\bar{D} - D}{s_{\bar{D}}} = \frac{-6 - 0}{2} = -3.00$$

Step 4: Make Decision. The t statistic is in the critical region. This is a very unlikely value for t if H_0 is true. Therefore, we reject H_0. The researcher concludes that the treatment does have a significant effect on performance scores.

HINTS AND CAUTIONS

1.   It is important to remember that the repeated measures analysis is based on difference scores (D scores). Therefore, the computations of s and $s_{\bar{D}}$ are based on the sample of D scores.

2.   When calculating the difference scores, be sure all of them are obtained by subtracting in the same direction. That is, you may use either 1st - 2nd, or 2nd - 1st as long as the same method is used throughout.

SELF-TEST AND REVIEW

1.   A related samples experiment can be either a "repeated measures" design or a "matched subjects" design. Briefly describe each of these experimental designs.

2.   The data for the repeated measures t statistic consist of the difference scores (Ds) that are obtained by measuring the amount of change that occurs between the first measurement and the second measurement for each subject. Usually the difference scores are computed so that an increase from the first to the second measurement produces a positive (+) difference, and a decrease from first to second measurement produces a negative (-) difference. The signs (+ and -) of the difference scores must be observed in all other calculations with the D values. Calculate the difference scores and the mean difference, $\bar{D}$, for the following sample.

Subject	1st	2nd	D
#1	8	10	
#2	6	12	
#3	10	7	
#4	9	17	
#5	7	14	

3.   The data for the repeated measures t statistic consist of difference scores, and the null hypothesis also concerns difference scores. In symbols and words, state the null hypothesis for the repeated measures hypothesis test.

4.   The t statistic for the repeated measures test has the same structure as the single-sample t statistic that we examined in Chapter 10. In terms of the formulas, the only difference between these two t statistics is that the single-sample formulas uses X (to stand for score) and the repeated measures formulas uses D (to stand for difference score). Degrees of freedom for these two t statistics are also computed in the same way.

   a.   For the data shown in problem 2, what would be the df for the repeated measures t statistic?

   b.   A researcher selects a sample of n = 10 individuals and measures each person's performance in two treatment conditions. If the results of this experiment are evaluated using a repeated measures t, what would be the df for the t statistic?

   c.   A researcher reports a t statistic with df = 19 for a repeated measures experiment comparing two treatment conditions. How many subjects participated in this experiment?

5.   One disadvantage of the repeated measures t is that it cannot be used to evaluate the difference in means between two distinct populations (such as men versus women). Another difficulty with a repeated measures experiment is that the researcher must be careful to avoid "carry-over" effects. Define a carry-over effect.

6.   In general, a repeated measures experiment is considered to be more precise or more powerful than an independent measures experiment. Briefly explain the advantage of a repeated measures study over an independent measures study.

7.   The repeated measures t statistic can be used for estimation as well as hypothesis testing. As usual with estimation, the t statistic formula is solved for the unknown population mean.

$$\mu_D = \bar{D} + ts_{\bar{D}}$$

The values of $\bar{D}$ and $s_{\bar{D}}$ are obtained directly from the sample data.
   a.   What value of t is used in this equation for a point estimate of the population mean difference?
   b.   What values of t would be used in the equation for a 90% confidence interval estimate of μ_D based on a sample of n = 15?

8.   A researcher assesses the effectiveness of relaxation training for treating migraine headaches. For a week prior to the training sessions, a sample of n = 9 subjects records the number of headaches they have. Immediately after completing a dozen training sessions the subjects again record the number of headaches they

have for one week. The results from this sample showed an average of three fewer headaches per week after training, $\bar{D} = -3$ with SS = 72.

    a. Do these data indicate that relaxation training has a significant effect on the number of migraine headaches? Test at the .05 level.

    b. Estimate the population mean difference (μ_D) resulting from relaxation training. Use an interval estimate so that you are 90% confident that the population mean difference is in your interval.

9. A manager would like to determine whether there is a significant improvement in sales staff productivity during their first 6 months of employment. For n = 16 new employees, the number of sales during the first month and during the sixth month are recorded. For each employee the manager computes the difference between these two figures. The sample of difference scores shows that sales increased an average of $\bar{D} = 8.5$ with SS = 6000 over the six months. Do these data indicate a significant improvement in sales performance with experience? Use a <u>one-tailed test</u> with $\alpha = .05$.

10. An educator would like to assess the effectiveness of a new instructional program for reading. The control group consists of 4 first graders who are provided with the traditional instruction used at the school. Another sample of 4 first graders receives the experimental instruction. The subjects in the experimental group are matched one-to-one in terms of IQ with the subjects in the control group. At the end of the year, both groups are tested with a standard reading exam. The data are as follows:

Matched Pair	Control	Experimental
A	10	12
B	15	25
C	13	15
D	18	20

On the basis of these data can the educator conclude that the special program has a significant effect on reading scores? Test at the .05 level.

ANSWERS TO SELF-TEST

1.   In a repeated measures design, the same sample is tested in each of the different treatment conditions. In a matched samples design, there is a different sample for each treatment but the individuals in the first sample are matched one-to-one with the individuals in the second sample.

2.

Subject	1st	2nd	D	
#1	8	10	+2	
#2	6	12	+6	$\Sigma D = 20$
#3	10	7	-3	
#4	9	17	+8	$\bar{D} = 20/5 = 4$
#5	7	14	+7	

3.   The null hypothesis says that the population mean difference is zero. The population mean difference is the average of the difference scores for all the individuals in the entire population. In symbols:

H_0: $\mu_D = 0$

4. a. With n = 5, df = 4
    b. df = 9
    c. With df = 19, n = 20

5. A carry-over effect occurs when a subject's participation in one treatment condition influences his/her performance in the next treatment condition. The effects of the first treatment carry over to the second treatment.

6. The repeated measures experiment eliminates individual differences as a source of error. This reduces the overall variability in the experiment and makes it easier to see a treatment effect if one exists.

7. a. For a point estimate, always use t = 0.
    b. With df = 14 and 90% confidence the t value would be 1.761.

8. a. The null hypothesis states that there is no effect, $\mu_D = 0$. With n = 9, df = 8 and the critical values are t = $\pm$2.306. For these data, t = -3.00. Reject H_0 and conclude that relaxation training has a significant effect on migraine headaches.
    b. For a 90% confidence interval use t = 1.860. The interval extends from -4.860 to -1.140. We conclude that the training does reduce headaches, and that the average reduction for the population is between 1.14 and 4.86 headaches per week.

9.   The manager is predicting an increase in
productivity.   The hypotheses are,
H_0: $\mu_D \leq 0$ (no increase)
H_1: $\mu_D > 0$ (increase)

With df = 15, the critical region consists of t values
greater than +1.753.   For these data, t = 1.70.   Fail to
reject H_0.   These data do not provide sufficient evidence
to conclude that there is an increase in productivity.

10.   The null hypothesis states that there is no
difference between the traditional program and the new
program.   With df = 3, the critical t value is 3.182.
For these data, $\bar{D}$ = 4, SS = 48, and t = 2.   Fail to
reject H_0.

CHAPTER **13** INTRODUCTION TO ANALYSIS OF VARIANCE

LEARNING OBJECTIVES

1.   You should be familiar with the purpose, terminology, and special notation of analysis of variance.

2.   You should be able to perform an analysis of variance for the data from a single-factor, independent measures experiment.

3.   You should recognize when post hoc tests are necessary and you should be able to complete an analysis of variance using Tukey's HSD or the Scheffe post hoc test.

4.   You should be able to report the results of an analysis of variance using either a summary table or an

F-ratio (including df values). Also, you should be able
to understand and interpret these reports when they
appear in scientific literature.

NEW TERMS AND CONCEPTS

The following terms were introduced in this chapter.
Define or describe each term and, where appropriate, describe
how each term is related to other terms in the list.

factor
levels of a factor
F-ratio
error term
MS (Mean Square)
post hoc test
a priori test
a posteriori test
between treatments SS, df, and MS
within treatments SS, df, and MS
total SS and df

NEW FORMULAS

$$SS_{total} = \Sigma X^2 - \frac{G^2}{N} \qquad\qquad df_{total} = N - 1$$

$$SS_{between} = \Sigma\frac{T^2}{n} - \frac{G^2}{N} \qquad\qquad df_{between} = k - 1$$

$$SS_{within} = \Sigma SS_{each\ treatment} \qquad df_{within} = N - k$$

$$MS_{between} = \frac{SS_{between}}{df_{between}} \qquad\qquad MS_{within} = \frac{SS_{within}}{df_{within}}$$

$$F = \frac{MS_{between}}{MS_{within}}$$

$$HSD = q\sqrt{\frac{MS_{within}}{n}}$$

Analysis of Variance: Analysis of variance is a hypothesis testing technique that is used to determine whether there are differences among the means of two or more populations. In this chapter we examined ANOVA for an independent measures experiment, which means that the data consist of a separate sample for each treatment condition (or each population). Before you begin the actual analysis, you should complete all the preliminary calculations with the data, including T and SS for each sample and G and ΣX^2 for the entire set of scores. The following example will be used to demonstrate ANOVA.

A researcher has obtained three different samples representing three populations. The data are presented below.

Sample 1	Sample 2	Sample 3	
0	6	6	
4	8	5	G = 60
0	5	9	
1	4	4	$\Sigma X^2 = 356$
0	2	6	
T = 5	T = 25	T = 30	
SS = 12	SS = 20	SS = 14	

<u>Step 1</u>: State the hypotheses and select an alpha level. The null hypothesis states that there are no mean differences among the three populations.

H_0: $\mu_1 = \mu_2 = \mu_3$

Remember, we generally do not try to list specific alternatives, but rather state a generic alternative hypothesis.

H_1: At least one population mean is different from the others

For this test we will use $\alpha = .05$.

<u>Step 2</u>: Locate the critical region. With k = 3 samples, the numerator of the F-ratio will have df = k-1 = 2. There are n = 5 scores in each sample. Within each sample there are n - 1 = 4 degrees of freedom, and summing across all three samples gives

df = 4 + 4 + 4 = 12

for the denominator of the F-ratio. Thus, the F-ratio for this analysis will have df = 2,12.

Sketch the entire distribution of F-ratios with df = 2,12 and locate the extreme 5% of the distribution. The critical F value is 3.88.

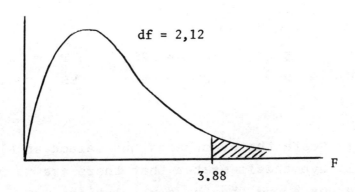

Step 3: Compute the test statistic. It is best to work through the calculations in a systematic way. Compute all three parts of the analysis (total, between, and within) and check that the two components add to the total.

$$SS_{total} = \Sigma X^2 - \frac{G^2}{N}$$

$$= 356 - \frac{(60)^2}{15}$$

$$= 356 - 240 = 116$$

$$SS_{between} = \Sigma \frac{T^2}{n} - \frac{G^2}{N}$$

$$= \frac{(5)^2}{5} + \frac{(25)^2}{5} + \frac{(30)^2}{5} - \frac{(60)^2}{15}$$

$$= 5 + 125 + 180 - 240 = 70$$

$$SS_{within} = \Sigma SS = 12 + 20 + 14 = 46$$
(Check that 116 = 70 + 46)

We have already found $df_{between}$ and df_{within}. To complete the analysis of df, compute

$$df_{total} = N - 1 = 15 - 1 = 14$$
(Check that 14 = 12 + 2)
Next, compute the two variances (Mean Squares) that will form the F-ratio.

$$MS_{between} = \frac{SS_{between}}{df_{between}}$$

$$= \frac{70}{2} = 35$$

$$MS_{within} = \frac{SS_{within}}{df_{within}}$$

$$= \frac{46}{12} = 3.83$$

Finally, the F-ratio for these data is,

$$F = \frac{MS_{between}}{MS_{within}} = \frac{35}{3.83} = 9.14$$

Step 4: Make decision. The F-ratio for these data is in the critical region. The numerator is more than 9 times larger than the denominator which indicates a significant treatment effect. Reject H_0 and conclude that there are differences among the means of the three populations.

HINTS AND CAUTIONS

1.   It may help you to understand analysis of variance if you remember that measuring variance is conceptually the same as measuring differences. The goal of the analysis is to determine whether the mean differences in the data are larger than would be expected by chance.

2.   The formulas for SS between treatments and SS within treatments, and their role in the F-ratio may be easier

to remember if you look at the similarities between the independent measures t formula and the F-ratio formula.

a. The numerator of the t statistic measures the difference between the two sample means, $(\bar{X}_1 - \bar{X}_2)$. The numerator of the F-ratio also looks at differences between treatments by computing the variability for the treatment totals.

b. The standard error in the denominator of the t statistic is computed by first pooling the two sample variances. This calculation uses the SS values from each of the two separate samples. The denominator of the F-ratio also uses the SS values from each of the separate samples to compute SS within treatments. In fact, when there are only two treatment conditions, the pooled variance from the t statistic is equivalent to the MS within treatments from the F-ratio.

SELF-TEST AND REVIEW

1. Analysis of variance (ANOVA) is a statistical technique used to test for differences among the means of two or more populations. If a researcher is comparing three different populations, state the null hypothesis for an analysis of variance.

2. Describe the conditions when you should use ANOVA instead of t tests and explain why t tests are not appropriate under these conditions.

3. The basic "analysis" in ANOVA involves partitioning total variability into two components.
   a. Identify the two components.
   b. Describe the sources of variability that

contribute to each of the two components.

4.   The test statistic for analysis of variance is an F-ratio which is a ratio of two sample variances.
     a.   Identify the two sample variances that make up the numerator and denominator of the F-ratio.
     b.   In ANOVA the sample variances in the F-ratio are identified by a special notation. Identify and explain this notation.

5.   On average, what value is expected for an F-ratio when the null hypothesis is true? Explain why this value is expected.

6.   Analysis of variance involves a great deal of special notation. Identify the significance of each of the following symbols.
     a.   n   b.   T   c.   N
     d.   G   e.   k

7.   In ANOVA, the variance between treatments $(MS_{between})$ provides a measure of the differences between the sample means. In the formula for $SS_{between}$ you usually use the sample totals (Ts) as the basis for computing the amount of variability (or differences) between treatment means. The denominator of the F-ratio, the variance within treatments (MS_{within}) provides a measure of the amount of variability (or differences) due to chance. The following data summarize the results of two experiments. Each experiment compares three treatment conditions, and each experiment uses separate samples of n = 10 for each treatment.

Experiment 1	Experiment 2

$$T_1 = 10 \quad T_2 = 15 \quad T_3 = 20 \qquad\qquad T_1 = 5 \quad T_2 = 20 \quad T_3 = 35$$

$$SS_1 = 40 \quad SS_2 = 40 \quad SS_3 = 40 \qquad SS_1 = 20 \quad SS_2 = 20 \quad SS_3 = 20$$

Just looking at the data - without doing any calculations - answer each of the fallowing questions.

    a. Which experiment will produce the larger $MS_{Between}$?

    b. Which experiment will produce the larger MS_{Within}?

    c. Which experiment will produce the larger F-ratio?

8.   Each F-ratio has two separate values for degrees of freedom: df for the variance in the numerator and df for the denominator.

    a. A researcher compares four treatment conditions using a sample of n = 5 in each treatment. If the data are evaluated using ANOVA, what would be the df for the F-ratio?

    b. A researcher reports an F-ratio with df = 2,30 for an independent measures experiment. How many treatment conditions were compared in this experiment, and how many individual subjects participated in the experiment?

9.   Briefly explain when post hoc tests are necessary and describe what information they provide.

10. The following data are from an independent measures experiment comparing three treatment conditions.

```
                    Treatments
          I        II        III
          1         6         4
          0         2         8
          4         1        10
          3         4         6
          2         2         7
```

    a. Do these data provide evidence for a significant difference among the three treatments? Test at the .05 level of significance.

    b. Use Tukey's HSD test to determine which treatments are significantly different and which are not.

11. The following data are from an independent measures experiment comparing two treatments. Without doing any calculations, you should be able to predict the outcome of an ANOVA for these data. Hint: How much difference is there between the two treatments?

```
          Treatment 1                Treatment 2
              1                           5
              2                           0
              4                           3
              1                           0
          T = 8                       T = 8
          SS = 6                      SS = 18
```

12. The following data are from three separate samples. Does it appear that these samples came from the same population or from different populations?

    a. Use an F-max test to determine whether there is

any evidence for a significant difference among the population variances. Test at the .05 level of significance.

b. Use an ANOVA to determine whether there is any evidence for a significant difference among the population means.

Sample 1	Sample 2	Sample 3
n = 6	n = 6	n = 6
$\bar{X}$ = 1	$\bar{X}$ = 3	$\bar{X}$ = 4
SS = 21	SS = 28	SS = 41

13. The following data are from two separate samples.

a. Use an analysis of variance with α = .05 to determine whether these data provide evidence for a significant difference between the two population means.

b. If you had used a t test instead of ANOVA, what value would you have obtained for the t statistic?

Sample 1	Sample 2
n = 10	n = 10
$\bar{X}$ = 3	$\bar{X}$ = 5
SS = 200	SS = 160

ANSWERS TO SELF-TEST

1. The null hypothesis states that there are no differences among the three population means. In symbols,

H_0: $\mu_1 = \mu_2 = \mu_3$

2. You should always use ANOVA instead of t tests when you are comparing more than two populations means. With only two populations you may use either ANOVA or t. With

more than two populations, you would need several t tests
to make all the comparisons and each test contributes to
the probability of a Type I error.

3.   a.   The total variability is partitioned into
variability between treatments and variability within
treatments.
     b.   Variability between treatments can be caused by:
1) treatment effect, 2) individual differences, and 3)
experimental error. The variability within treatments
can be caused by 1) individual differences and 2)
experimental error.

4.   a.   The numerator is the variance (MS) between
treatments, and the denominator is the variance (MS)
within treatments.
     b.   In ANOVA, variances are called Mean Squares or
MSs. The term refers to the fact that variance is the
mean squared deviation.

5.   When H_0 is true, the F-ratio is expected to be near
1.00. This fact is a result of the structure of the F-
ratio formula,

$$F = \frac{\text{treatment effect} + \text{individual diffs.} + \text{experimental error}}{\text{individual diffs.} + \text{experimental error}}$$

When H_0 is true and the treatment effect is zero, so the
numerator and denominator are measuring the same
variance.

6.   a.   The number of scores in each treatment condition
is n.
     b.   The sum of the scores for each treatment
condition is T.
     c.   The total number of scores in the experiment is

N.

   d. The sum of all of the scores in the experiment
is G.

   e. The number of different treatment conditions is
k.

7. a. Experiment 2 will produce the larger $MS_{between}$
because there are larger differences between the
treatment totals.

   b. Experiment 1 will produce the larger MS_{within}
because the SS values are larger within each treatment
condition.

   c. Experiment 2 will produce the larger F-ratio
because the F will have a larger numerator and a smaller
denominator than in Experiment 1.

8. a. There are 3 degrees of freedom between
treatments and 16 degrees of freedom within treatments.
The F-ratio has df = 3,16.

   b. There are 3 treatment conditions with a total of
N = 33 subjects in the three samples.

9. Post hoc tests are done after an analysis of
variance with more than two treatments, and where H_0 is
rejected. The ANOVA concludes that there are differences
among the treatments and the post tests are used to find
which treatments are different.

10. a.

Source	SS	df	MS	
Between Treatments	70	2	35	F = 9.13
Within Treatments	46	12	3.83	
Total	116	14		

   b. Tukey's HSD = 3.30. By this standard,

treatment III is significantly different from both
treatment I and treatment II. The difference between
treatments I and II is not significant.

11. For these data there is no difference between the
two treatments: Both totals are T = 8 and both
treatments have a mean of $\bar{X}$ = 2. $SS_{between}$ is zero and
the F-ratio is zero.

12. a. For these data, F-max = 1.95. This value is not
large enough to indicate any significant differences
among the population variances.

b.

Source	SS	df	MS	
Between Treatments	12	2	6	F = 1.00
Within Treatments	90	15	6	
Total	102	17		

13. a. With df = 1,18 the critical value for F is 4.41.
For these data,

Source	SS	df	MS	
Between Treatments	20	1	20	F = 1.00
Within Treatments	360	18	20	
Total	380	19		

Fail to reject H_0.

b. The t test would produce a t statistic of
$t = \sqrt{F}$ = 1.00.

CHAPTER 14

REPEATED MEASURES ANALYSIS OF VARIANCE

LEARNING OBJECTIVES

1.   Be able to explain the logic of the repeated measures ANOVA.

2.   Understand how variability is partitioned and what sources of variability contribute to each component.

3.   Know the difference between the analysis for repeated versus independent measures designs.

4.   Be able to perform the computations for a complete analysis.

NEW TERMS AND CONCEPTS

The following terms were introduced in this chapter. Define or describe each term and, where appropriate, describe how each term is related to other terms in the list.

between treatments variability
within treatments variability
between subjects variability
error variability
treatment effect
individual differences
experimental error
F-ratio

NEW FORMULAS

In addition to the total SS, between treatments SS, within treatments SS, and the corresponding df and MS values that were presented in Chapter 13, several new formulas are introduced in Chapter 14:

$$SS_{\text{bet. subjects}} = \Sigma\frac{P^2}{k} - \frac{G^2}{N}$$

$$df_{\text{bet. subjects}} = n - 1$$

$$SS_{\text{error}} = SS_{\text{within}} - SS_{\text{bet. subjects}}$$

$$df_{\text{error}} = (N - k) - (n - 1)$$

$$F = \frac{MS_{\text{bet. treatments}}}{MS_{\text{error}}}$$

The repeated measures ANOVA is used to determine whether there are any differences among the means of two or more different treatments using the data from a single sample that has been measured in each treatment condition. The calculations and notation for the repeated measures ANOVA are very similar to the independent measures design. In fact, the first stage of the repeated measures analysis is identical to the independent ANOVA. However, the repeated analysis continues through a second stage where the individual differences are removed from the denominator of the F-ratio. The following example will be used to demonstrate the repeated measures ANOVA.

A researcher is comparing four different treatment conditions using a repeated measures experiment with a sample of n = 6 subjects. The data from this experiment are as follows:

Subject	Treatment 1	2	3	4	P
#1	0	2	6	0	8
#2	4	0	7	1	12
#3	5	4	11	0	20
#4	8	7	13	4	32
#5	7	2	9	2	20
#6	6	3	14	5	28
T	30	18	60	12	
SS	40	28	52	22	

$$G = 120 \qquad \Sigma X^2 = 970$$

Step 1: State the hypotheses and select an alpha level. The null hypothesis states that there are no

differences among the means for the four treatment
conditions.

H_0: $\mu_1 = \mu_2 = \mu_3 = \mu_4$

The general alternative hypothesis is,

H_1: At least one of the treatment means is
different from the others.

We will use $\alpha = .05$.

Step 2: Locate the critical region. The first problem
is to determine the df values for the F-ratio. We will
conduct a complete analysis of df to determine $df_{between}$
and df_{error}. For these data,

$$df_{total} = N - 1 = 24 - 1 = 23$$
$$df_{between} = k - 1 = 4 - 1 = 3$$
$$df_{within} = N - k = 24 - 4 = 20$$

This completes the first stage of the analysis. (Check
to be sure that the total equals the sum of the two
components.) For the second stage,

$$df_{subjects} = n - 1 = 6 - 1 = 5$$
$$df_{error} = df_{within} - df_{subjects}$$
$$= 20 - 5$$
$$= 15$$

The F-ratio will have df = 3, 15. Sketch the entire
distribution of F-ratios with df = 3,15 and locate the
extreme 5% of the distribution. The critical F value is
3.29.

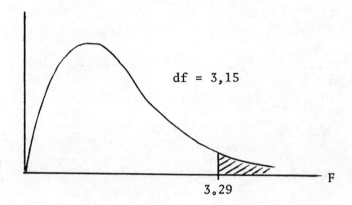

df = 3,15

3.29

F

<u>Step 3</u>: Compute the test statistic. We have completed
the analysis for df, so we will continue with the
analysis of SS. As before, we will complete the analysis
in two stages.

$$SS_{total} = \Sigma X^2 - \frac{G^2}{N}$$

$$= 970 - \frac{(120)^2}{24}$$

$$= 970 - 600 = 370$$

$$SS_{between} = \Sigma \frac{T^2}{n} - \frac{G^2}{N}$$

$$= \frac{(30)^2}{6} + \frac{(18)^2}{6} + \frac{(60)^2}{6} + \frac{(12)^2}{6} - \frac{(120)^2}{24}$$

$$= 828 - 600 = 228$$

$$SS_{within} = \Sigma SS = 40 + 28 + 52 + 22 = 142$$

This completes the first stage. (Check to be sure that
the two components add to the total.) Continuing with
the second stage,

$$SS_{subjects} = \Sigma \frac{P^2}{k} - \frac{G^2}{N}$$

$$= \frac{8^2}{4} + \frac{12^2}{4} + \frac{20^2}{4} + \frac{32^2}{4} + \frac{20^2}{4} + \frac{28^2}{4} - \frac{120^2}{24}$$

$$= 704 - 600 = 104$$

$$SS_{error} = SS_{within} - SS_{subjects}$$

$$= 142 - 104$$

$$= 38$$

Next, compute the two Mean Squares that will form the F-ratio.

$$MS_{between} = \frac{SS_{between}}{df_{between}} = 228/3 = 76$$

$$MS_{error} = \frac{SS_{error}}{df_{error}} = 38/15 = 2.53$$

Finally, the F-ratio for these data is,

$$F = \frac{MS_{between}}{MS_{error}} = 76/2.53 = 30$$

Step 4: Make decision. The F-ratio for these data is in the critical region. This is a very unlikely value to be obtained if H_0 is true. Therefore, we reject H_0 and conclude that there are significant differences among the four treatment means.

HINTS AND CAUTIONS

1. In the repeated measures ANOVA, it is important that you remember to use the correct error term (denominator) for the F-ratio, namely MS_{error}.

2. A very common mistake when locating the critical region for a repeated measure F-ratio is to use within treatments df. Remember, the correct df value for the error term is the error df.

3. One important fact that may help you to remember the structure and the value of a repeated measures ANOVA is that the repeated measures design eliminates individual differences. The individual differences do not exist in the numerator of the F-ratio because the same individuals are used in all of the treatment conditions. In the denominator of the F-ratio there are no individual differences because they are subtracted out in the second stage of the analysis.

4. In the typical display of data for a repeated measures experiment the scores for each subject are listed in rows and the scores for each treatment are listed in columns (see the Step-by-Step example). When you are computing $SS_{between}$ you are measuring the differences between columns of data. When you compute $SS_{subjects}$ you are measuring the differences between rows of data.

   This observation should help you recognize the similarity between the formulas for these two SS values.

$$SS_{between} = \Sigma\frac{T^2}{n} - \frac{G^2}{N}$$

T = column total
n = number in each column

$$SS_{subjects} = \Sigma\frac{P^2}{k} - \frac{G^2}{N}$$

P = row total
k = number in each row

1. The repeated measures analysis of variance is intended for situations where a single sample of individuals is tested in two or more treatment conditions. The purpose of the analysis is to determine whether there are any differences among the means of the treatment conditions. In symbols and in words, state the null hypothesis for the repeated measures ANOVA (assume that there are 3 treatment conditions).

2. The analysis for a repeated measures design proceeds in two stages. The first stage is identical to the analysis for an independent measures design: the total variability is partitioned into variability between treatments and variability within treatments.
    a. Identify the sources of variability for each of the two components in the first stage of the analysis (between and within).
    b. Explain why the two components that result from the first stage of the analysis are not appropriate for an F-ratio.

3. In the second stage of the repeated measures analysis the variability within treatments is partitioned into two components.
    a. Identify the two components that result from the analysis of the within treatments variability.
    b. Explain why this second stage of analysis is necessary.

4. The final F-ratio in the repeated measures analysis is structured so that it has an expected value of 1.00 when the null hypothesis is true.

a. What sources of variability contribute to the numerator of the F-ratio ($MS_{between}$)?

b. Explain why "individual differences" is not listed as a source of variability in the numerator.

c. What sources of variability contribute to the denominator of the F-ratio (MS_{error})?

d. Explain why "individual differences" is not listed as a source of variability in the denominator.

5. There are two separate values for degrees of freedom for the F-ratio (one for the numerator and one for the denominator).

a. If a researcher uses a sample of n = 10 subjects in a repeated measures experiment comparing 3 treatment conditions, identify the df values for the F-ratio.

b. A researcher reports an F-ratio with df = 2,8 for a repeated measures experiment. How many treatment conditions were compared in this experiment and how many individual subjects participated in the experiment?

6. An industrial researcher tests 3 different keyboard designs for a new computer to determine which one produces optimal performance. Four computer operators are given text material and are told to type the material as fast as they can. They spend 3 minutes on each keyboard with a 5 minute rest between each trial. The number of errors committed are recorded. Do the following data indicate a significant difference among the 3 keyboard types? Test at the .05 level of significance.

Operator	1	2	3	P	
#1	6	2	4	12	
#2	8	6	7	21	
#3	3	6	9	18	$\Sigma X^2 = 360$
#4	3	2	4	9	
T	20	16	24		G = 60
SS	18	16	18		

7.   A sample of n = 7 individuals is selected to participate in a learning study. Each individual is tested at five different stages during learning (after 1 hour, 2 hours, 3 hours, etc.). The data from this experiment were examined using a repeated measures ANOVA to determine whether there was any evidence of a practice effect. The results are presented in the following summary table. Complete all the missing values in the table. Hint: Begin with the df column.

Source	SS	df	MS	
Between Treatments	___	___	10	F = ___
Within Treatments	___	___		
Between Subjects	52	___		
Error	___	___	___	
Total	140	___		

8.   A toy manufacturer is testing 3 versions of a toy that is under development. Among other things, the manufacturer would like to see which version of the toy attracts the most attention. A psychologist allows a child to play with all 3 toys and records the amount of time (in minutes) spent playing with each. A sample of n

= 5 children is used. Use the following data to determine whether there is a significant preference among the three toys. Use the .05 level of significance.

Child	Toy 1	Toy 2	Toy 3
A	0	2	4
B	2	2	8
C	3	1	5
D	0	3	6
E	0	2	7

ANSWERS TO SELF-TEST

1.   The null hypothesis states that there are no differences among the three population means for the different treatment conditions. In symbols,

$$H_0: \quad \mu_1 = \mu_2 = \mu_3$$

2.   a. Variability between treatments can be caused by a) treatment effect and b) experimental error. (there are no individual differences because the same individuals are used in all treatments.) The variability within treatments can be caused by a) individual differences and b) experimental error.

       b. In an F-ratio the numerator and the denominator should have identical sources of variability when the null hypothesis is true (when there is no treatment effect).

3.   a.   The variability within treatments is partitioned into variability between subjects (individual differences) and variability due to error.

   b.   The second stage is necessary to obtain a denominator for the F-ratio that contains only experimental error (no individual differences).

4.   a.   The numerator of the F-ratio contains variability from treatment effects and experimental error.

   b.   There are no individual differences in the variability between treatments because the same individuals are used in every treatment.

   c.   The denominator of the F-ratio contains variability from experimental error.

   d.   There are no individual differences in the denominator because they are subtracted out in the second stage of the analysis.

5.   a.   The between treatments MS would have df = 2, and the error MS would have df = 18. The F-ratio has df = 2,18.

   b.   The experiment compared 3 treatments using a sample of n = 5 subjects.

6.   The null hypothesis states that there are no differences among the three keyboard types. With df = 2,6 the critical value is F = 5.14.

Source	SS	df	MS	
Between Treatments	8	2	4	F = 1.09
Within Treatments	52	9		
Between Subjects	30	3		
Error	22	6	3.67	
Total	60	11		

Fail to reject H_0. There are no significant differences among the three keyboard types.

7.

Source	SS	df	MS	
Between Treatments	40	4	10	F = 5.00
Within Treatments	100	30		
Between Subjects	52	6		
Error	48	24	2	
Total	140	34		

8. The null hypothesis states that there are no differences among the 3 toys. With df = 2,8, the critical boundary is F = 4.46.

Source	SS	df	MS	
Between Treatments	70	2	35	F = 20
Within Treatments	20	12		
Between Subjects	6	4		
Error	14	8	1.75	
Total	90	14		

Reject the null hypothesis and conclude that there are significant differences among the three toys.

CHAPTER **15** TWO–FACTOR ANALYSIS OF VARIANCE
(INDEPENDENT MEASURES)

LEARNING OBJECTIVES

1.   Be able to conduct a two-factor ANOVA to evaluate
the data from an independent measures experiment that
uses two independent variables.

2.   Understand the definition of an interaction between
two factors, and be able to recognize an interaction from
a description or a graph of experimental results.

3.   Be familiar with the use of a two-factor design as a
means of controlling variability within treatments.

NEW TERMS AND CONCEPTS

The following terms were introduced in this chapter. Define or describe each term and, where appropriate, describe how each term is related to other terms in the list.

two-factor experiment
matrix and cells
main effect
interaction
factor A
factor B
p   (number of levels of factor A)
q   (number of levels of factor B)

NEW FORMULAS

$$SS_{between\ cells} = \Sigma\frac{AB^2}{n} - \frac{G^2}{N}$$

$$df_{between\ cells} = pq - 1$$

$$SS_A = \Sigma\frac{A^2}{qn} - \frac{G^2}{N} \qquad\qquad df_A = p - 1$$

$$SS_B = \Sigma\frac{B^2}{pn} - \frac{G^2}{N} \qquad\qquad df_B = q - 1$$

$$SS_{AxB} = SS_{between\ cells} - SS_A - SS_B \qquad df_{AxB} = (df_A)(df_B)$$

Two-Factor ANOVA. The two-factor analysis of variance is used for experimental data with two independent variables. The two factors are generally identified as A and B, and the data are presented in a matrix with the levels of factor A determining the rows and the levels of factor B determining the columns. The analysis of variance evaluates three separate hypotheses: one concerning the main effect of factor A, one concerning the main effect of factor B, and one concerning the interaction. In this chapter we considered the two-factor analysis for an independent measures experiment which means that the data consist of a separate sample for each AB treatment combination. The following example will be used to demonstrate the two-factor ANOVA.

The data below are from a two-factor experiment with p = 2 levels of factor A and q = 3 levels of factor B. There are n = 10 subjects in each treatment condition.

Factor B

		B1	B2	B3	
		AB = 10	AB = 20	AB = 30	A1 = 60
	A1	SS = 20	SS = 32	SS = 35	
Factor A					
	A2	AB = 10	AB = 10	AB = 10	A2 = 30
		SS = 15	SS = 35	SS = 25	
		B1 = 20	B2 = 30	B3 = 40	G = 90

$$\Sigma X^2 = 332$$

Step 1: State the hypotheses and select an alpha level. Because the two-factor ANOVA evaluates three separate hypotheses, there will be three null hypotheses, each with its own H_0.

For Factor A: H_0: $\mu_{A1} = \mu_{A2}$ (no A-effect)

H_1: $\mu_{A1} \neq \mu_{A2}$

For Factor B: H_0: $\mu_{B1} = \mu_{B2} = \mu_{B3}$ (no B-effect)

H_1:   At least one of the B means is different from the others

For AxB: H_0:   There is no interaction between factors A and B. That is, the effect of either factor does not depend on the levels of the other factor.

H_1: There is an A x B interaction

We will use $\alpha = .05$ for all three levels.

Step 2: Locate the critical regions. Because there are three separate tests, each with its own F-ratio, we will need to determine the critical region for each test separately. We begin by analyzing the degrees of freedom for these data to determine df for each F. The analysis proceeds in two stages.

df_{total} $= N - 1 = 60 - 1 = 59$
$df_{bet\ cells}$ $= pq - 1 = 6 - 1 = 5$
df_{within} $= N - pq = 60 - 6 = 54$

This completes the first stage of the analysis. (Check to be certain that the two components add to the total.) Continuing with the second stage,

$$df_A = p - 1 = 2 - 1 = 1$$
$$df_B = q - 1 = 3 - 1 = 2$$
$$df_{AxB} = (df_A)(df_B) = 1(2) = 2$$

Again, check to be certain that the three components from the second stage add to $df_{bet\ cells}$.

For these data, factor A will have an F-ratio with df = 1,54. Factor B and the AxB interaction both will have F-ratios with df = 2,54. Thus, we need F distributions and critical regions for two separate df values. Sketch the two distributions and locate the extreme 5% in each.

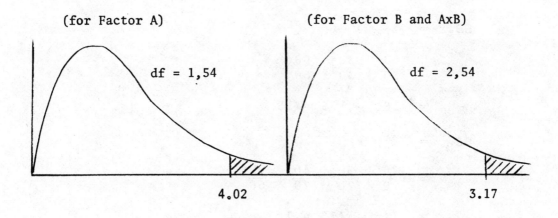

(for Factor A)

df = 1,54

4.02

(for Factor B and AxB)

df = 2,54

3.17

Step 3: Calculate the test statistic. Again, we will need three separate F-ratios. We already have analyzed the degrees of freedom for these data, so we will continue with the analysis of SS. As before, the analysis proceeds in two stages.

$$SS_{total} = \Sigma X^2 - \frac{G^2}{N}$$

$$= 332 - \frac{90^2}{60}$$

$$= 332 - 135 = 197$$

$$SS_{bet\ cells} = \Sigma \frac{AB^2}{n} - \frac{G^2}{N}$$

$$= \frac{10^2}{10} + \frac{20^2}{10} + \frac{30^2}{10} + \frac{10^2}{10} + \frac{10^2}{10} + \frac{10^2}{10} - \frac{90^2}{60}$$

$$= 170 - 135 = 35$$

$$SS_{within} = \Sigma SS = 20 + 32 + 35 + 15 + 35 + 25$$

$$= 162$$

This completes stage one. Be sure that the two components add to the total. For the second stage,

$$SS_A = \Sigma \frac{A^2}{qn} - \frac{G^2}{N}$$

$$= \frac{60^2}{30} + \frac{30^2}{30} - \frac{90^2}{60}$$

$$= 150 - 135 = 15$$

$$SS_B = \Sigma \frac{B^2}{pn} - \frac{G^2}{N}$$

$$= \frac{20^2}{20} + \frac{30^2}{20} + \frac{40^2}{20} - \frac{90^2}{60}$$

$$= 145 - 135 = 10$$

$$SS_{AxB} = SS_{bet\ cells} - SS_A - SS_B$$

$$= 35 - 15 - 10$$

$$= 10$$

Again, check that these three components from stage two add to $SS_{bet\ cells}$.

Next, compute the MS values that will comprise the three F-ratios.

$$MS_A = \frac{SS_A}{df_A} = 15/1 = 15$$

$$MS_B = \frac{SS_B}{df_B} = 10/2 = 5$$

$$MS_{AxB} = \frac{SS_{AxB}}{df_{AxB}} = 10/2 = 5$$

All three F-ratios will have the same error term (denominator):

$$MS_{within} = \frac{SS_{within}}{df_{within}} = 162/54 = 3$$

Finally, the three F-ratios are,

For Factor A: $F = \frac{MS_A}{MS_{within}} = 15/3 = 5$

For Factor B: $F = \frac{MS_B}{MS_{within}} = 5/3 = 1.67$

For AxB: $F = \frac{MS_{AxB}}{MS_{within}} = 5/3 = 1.67$

Step 4: Make decision. The F-ratio for Factor A is in the critical region. Therefore, we reject this H_0 and conclude there there is a significant difference between the mean for A1 and the mean for A2. The F-ratios for factor B and for the AxB interaction are not in the critical region. Therefore, we conclude that there is no significant main effect for factor B, and the data are not sufficient to conclude that there is an interaction between factors A and B.

1.   You should note that several of the SS formulas in the two-factor ANOVA have the same basic structure. Recognizing this structure can make it much easier to learn the formulas. For example, three of the SS formulas are computing variability due to differences between "things." These "things" and the corresponding SS values are:

SS_A (between levels of factor A)

SS_B (between levels of factor B)

$SS_{bet\ cells}$ (between treatment conditions or cells)

The first term of each SS formula involves squaring a total and dividing by the number of scores that were added to compute the total. For example, SS_A squares each of the A totals and divides by qn which is the number of scores used to find each A total. The second term in each of these SS formulas is G^2/N. Thus, all three of these formulas have the same structure that was used to compute SS between treatments for the single-factor ANOVA:

$$SS_{between} = \Sigma \frac{T^2}{n} - \frac{G^2}{N}$$

Note: You also could consider SS_{total} as measuring differences between scores. In this case each score is its own total, and n = 1, so the formula for SS_{total} also fits this same general structure.

Also note that the degrees of freedom associated with each of these SS values can be determined by simply

counting the number of "things" (or totals) and
subtracting 1.

2.   Remember that the F-ratios for factor A, factor B,
and the AxB interaction can all have different values for
df and therefore may have different critical values. Be
sure that you use the appropriate critical region for
each individual F-ratio.

SELF-TEST AND REVIEW

1.   In ANOVA an independent variable is referred to as a
factor. A two-factor experiment is one which has two
independent variables.
        a.   In the general notation of two-factor ANOVA, how
are the two factors identified?
        b.   The individual treatment conditions that make up
a factor are called the levels of the factor. What
notation is used to identify the number of levels of each
factor in a two-factor ANOVA?

2.   Combining two independent variables in a single
experiment has several advantages over examining the
variables with two separate experiments. First, the two
factor experiment is more economical in that it uses
fewer subjects. Also, the second factor can be used to
identify and control a source of variability and thereby
increase the chances of obtaining a significant F-ratio.
The greatest advantage of a two-factor experiment is the
opportunity to evaluate the interaction between the two
factors.
        a.   Define an interaction.

b. How does an interaction appear in a graph showing the results of a two-factor experiment?

3. The data from a two-factor experiment are usually presented in a matrix with the levels of one factor defining the rows and the levels of the second factor defining the columns. Each cell in the matrix corresponds to a unique treatment condition comprised of a specific level of Factor A combined with a specific level of Factor B. The two-factor ANOVA proceeds in two stages. In the first stage, the total variability is partitioned into two components: between cells and within cells (also called between treatments and within treatments). What happens in the second stage of the analysis?

4. The analysis of variance for a two-factor experiment produces three separate F-ratios evaluating three null hypotheses. Two hypotheses concern main effects and the third concerns the interaction.
   a. Define a main effect.
   b. State the three null hypotheses that are evaluated by a two-factor ANOVA.
   c. All three F-ratios use the same error term (denominator). What is this error term?

5. Briefly explain the process by which you find SS for the AxB interaction.

6. As always in the analysis of variance each F-ratio is a ratio of two sample variances called Mean Squares (MSs). Thus, each F-ratio has two values for df - one for the variance in the numerator and one for the variance in the denominator. For an experiment involving

3 levels of factor A and 4 levels of factor B with a
sample of n = 5 in each treatment condition,

     a. What are the df values for the F-ratio for
factor A?

     b. What are the df values for the F-ratio for
factor B?

     c. What are the df values for the F-ratio for the
interaction?

7.   Use a two-factor analysis of variance to evaluate
the following data from an independent measures
experimental design.

<table>
<tr><td></td><td colspan="3" align="center">Factor B</td></tr>
<tr><td></td><td align="center">B1</td><td align="center">B2</td><td align="center">B3</td></tr>
<tr><td rowspan="5" align="center">A1</td><td align="center">1</td><td align="center">3</td><td align="center">0</td></tr>
<tr><td align="center">0</td><td align="center">6</td><td align="center">0</td></tr>
<tr><td align="center">3</td><td align="center">4</td><td align="center">3</td></tr>
<tr><td align="center">1</td><td align="center">3</td><td align="center">2</td></tr>
<tr><td align="center">0</td><td align="center">4</td><td align="center">0</td></tr>
<tr><td rowspan="5" align="center">A2</td><td align="center">7</td><td align="center">2</td><td align="center">6</td></tr>
<tr><td align="center">6</td><td align="center">3</td><td align="center">8</td></tr>
<tr><td align="center">6</td><td align="center">0</td><td align="center">4</td></tr>
<tr><td align="center">4</td><td align="center">3</td><td align="center">4</td></tr>
<tr><td align="center">2</td><td align="center">2</td><td align="center">3</td></tr>
</table>

Factor A

8.   A researcher is evaluating two gasoline additives
which are designed to improve gas mileage. For a
particular model of test car, each additive by itself has
been shown to increase mileage by an average of 5 miles
per gallon. the researcher is interested in determining

the effect of combining the two additives.

a. One hypothesis the researcher is testing states that when the two additives are combined their separate effects will add together. The result should be a total improvement of 10 miles per gallon. The predicted results from this hypothesis are displayed in the following table.

Average mpg obtained for
different combinations of two gasoline additives

Additive B

		No	Yes
	No	25	30
Additive A			
	Yes	30	35

In terms of an analysis of variance, what outcome is predicted by this hypothesis? What main effects should be significant? What about the interaction?

b. Another hypothesis is that combining the two additives will not produce any better mileage than would be obtained with either additive alone. The predicted results from this hypothesis are displayed in the following table.

Additive B

		No	Yes
	No	25	30
Additive A			
	Yes	30	30

In terms of an analysis of variance, what outcome is predicted by this hypothesis?

9.   Suppose the researcher from problem 8 collected data on gas mileage to test the hypotheses about the two gas additives. Assume that a separate sample of cars was used in each treatment condition and the researcher obtained the data summarized in the following table.

    a.   Use an ANOVA to evaluate these data.

    b.   Does additive A have a significant effect? What about additive B? Describe how the combination of additives affects gas mileage.

                      Additive B
                  No   Yes

		No	Yes
Additive A	No	n = 4, $\bar{X}$ = 1, SS = 1	n = 4, $\bar{X}$ = 3, SS = 2
	Yes	n = 4, $\bar{X}$ = 3, SS = 2	n = 4, $\bar{X}$ = 3, SS = 1

Caution: The data show means, not totals.

For these data, x^2 = 118

ANSWERS TO SELF-TEST

1.   a.   The two factors are identified as A and B.

    b.   The number of levels of factor A is identified as p, and the number of levels for factor B is q.

2.   a.   An interaction exists when the effect on one factor depends on the levels of the second factor.

    b.   In a graph, an interaction appears as non-parallel lines.

3.   In the second stage of the two-factor ANOVA, the variability between treatments is partitioned into 1) variability due to factor A, 2) variability due to factor B, and 3) variability from the AxB interaction.

4.   a.   A main effect is the overall mean difference among the levels of one factor, averaging over the levels of the second factor.
      b.   The three null hypotheses evaluated in a two-factor ANOVA are:
            1)   There is no main effect for factor A.
            2)   There is no main effect for factor B.
            3)   There is no AxB interaction.
      c.   All three F-ratios use the MS within treatments as the error term.

5.   The SS for the AxB interaction is not computed directly. Instead, you compute SS between treatments and then subtract the SS for factor A and the SS for factor B.

6.   a.   Factor A has df = 2,48.
      b.   Factor B has df = 3,48.
      c.   The AxB interaction has df = 6,48.

7.

Source	SS	df	MS	
Between Treatments	90	5		
Factor A	30	1	30	F = 12.41
Factor B	0	2	0	F = 0
AxB	60	2	30	F = 12.41
Within Treatments	58	24	2.42	
Total	148	29		

8.   a.   IF the effects of the two "factors" add together, there should be no interaction. Each of the individual factors should be significant.

   b.   If the two factors do not add, there should be an interaction. The individual main effects probably would still be significant but the interaction could affect the magnitude of the main effects.

9.   a.   All F-ratios have df = 1,12 and all have the same critical value, F = 4.75.

Source	SS	df	MS	
Between Treatments	12	3		
Factor A	4	1	4	F = 8
Factor B	4	1	4	F = 8
AxB	4	1	4	F = 8
Within Treatments	6	12	0.5	
Total	18	15		

   b.   Additive A and additive B both have a significant effect on mileage. However the effects of the two separate additives do not add (there is an interaction). The combination of the two additives is no more effective than either additive alone.

CHAPTER 16 CORRELATION AND REGRESSION

LEARNING OBJECTIVES

1.   Understand the Pearson correlation and what aspects
of a relationship it measures.

2.   Know the uses and limitations of measures of
correlation.

3.   Be able to compute the Pearson correlation by the
regular formula (using either the definitional or
computational formula for SP) or by the z-score formula.

4.   Be able to use a sample correlation to evaluate a
hypothesis about the correlation for the general
population.

5.   Recognize the general form of a linear equation and be able to identify its slope and Y-intercept.

6.   Be able to compute the linear regression equation for a set of data.

7.   Be able to use the regression equation to compute a predicted value of Y for any given value of X.

8.   Be able to compute the standard error of estimate for a regression equation and understand exactly what is measured by this standard error.

NEW TERMS AND CONCEPTS

The following terms were introduced in this chapter. Define or describe each term and, where appropriate, describe how each term is related to other terms in the list.

positive relationship
negative relationship
perfect relationship
Pearson correlation
significance of a correlation
linear relationship
sum of products
restricted range
coefficient of determination
linear equation
slope
Y-intercept
regression equation for Y
standard error of estimate

NEW FORMULAS

$$SP = \Sigma(X - \overline{X})(Y - \overline{Y})$$

$$SP = \Sigma XY - \frac{\Sigma X \Sigma Y}{n}$$

$$r = \frac{SP}{\sqrt{SS_x SS_y}}$$

$$r = \frac{\Sigma z_x z_y}{n}$$

$$\hat{Y} = bX + a$$

$$\text{where} \quad b = \frac{SP}{SS_x} \quad \text{and} \quad a = \overline{Y} - b\overline{X}$$

STEP--BY-STEP

The following example will be used to demonstrate the calculation of the Pearson correlation and the regression equation.

A researcher has pairs of scores (X and Y values) for a sample of n = 5 subjects. The data are as follows:

Person	X	Y
#1	0	-2
#2	2	-5
#3	8	14
#4	6	3
#5	4	0

Step 1: Sketch a scatterplot of the data and make a preliminary estimate of the correlation. Also, sketch a line through the middle of the data points and note the slope and Y-intercept of the line.

For these data, there appears to be a fairly good, positive correlation - probably around r = +.7 or +.8. The line has a positive slope and appears to intersect the Y-axis about 5 points below zero.

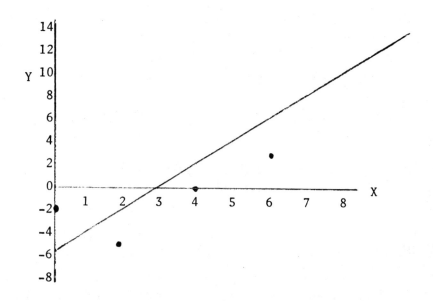

<u>Step 2</u>:   To compute the Pearson correlation you must find SS for both X and Y as well as SP.   These same values are needed to find the regression equation.   If both sets of scores (X and Y) have means that are whole numbers, then you may use the definitional formulas for SS and SP. Otherwise, it is better to use the computational formulas.   Although these data have X̄ = 4 and Ȳ = 2, we will demonstrate the computational formulas.

Using one large table, list the X and Y values in the first two columns, then continue with the squared values and the XY products.   Find the sum of the numbers in each column.   These sums are needed to find SS and SP.

X	Y	X^2	Y^2	XY
0	-2	0	4	0
2	-5	4	25	-10
8	14	64	196	112
6	3	36	9	18
4	0	16	0	0
20	10	120	234	120 (sums)

Use the sums from the table to compute SS for X and Y, and SP.

For X: $SS = \Sigma X^2 - \dfrac{(\Sigma X)^2}{n}$ $= 120 - \dfrac{(20)^2}{5}$

$$= 120 - 80$$
$$= 40$$

For Y: $SS = \Sigma Y^2 - \dfrac{(\Sigma Y)^2}{n}$ $= 234 - \dfrac{(10)^2}{5}$

$$= 234 - 20$$
$$= 214$$

and $SP = \Sigma XY - \dfrac{\Sigma X \Sigma Y}{n}$ $= 120 - \dfrac{(20)(10)}{5}$

$$= 120 - 40$$
$$= 80$$

Step 3: Compute the Pearson correlation and compare the answer with your preliminary estimate from Step 1. For these data,

$$r = \frac{SP}{\sqrt{SS_x SS_y}}$$

$$= \frac{80}{\sqrt{(40)(214)}}$$

$$= \frac{80}{\sqrt{8560}}$$

$$= .865$$

The obtained correlation, $r = +0.865$ agrees with our preliminary estimate.

Step 4: Compute the values for the regression equation, and compare the obtained equation with the preliminary estimates made in Step 1. The general form of the regression equation is,

$$\hat{Y} = bX + a$$

For these data,

$$b = \frac{SP}{SS_x} = \frac{80}{40} = 2$$

and $a = \bar{Y} - b\bar{X}$
$$= 2 - 2(4)$$
$$= -6$$

The regression equation is: $\hat{Y} = 2X - 6$

Both the slope constant (b = +2) and the Y-intercept (a = -6) agree with our preliminary estimates.

HINTS AND CAUTIONS

1.   Remember, a correlation of -1.00 indicates a perfect fit, too. The sign indicates the direction of the relationship, not its magnitude.

2.   Remember that n refers to the number of individuals (pairs of scores).

3.   The formula for the Y-intercept (a) in the regression equation may be easier to remember if you note that this formula simply guarantees that the point defined by ($\bar{X}$, $\bar{Y}$) is on the regression line. Thus, when X = $\bar{X}$, the predicted Y score will be $\bar{Y}$. In the equation,
$$\bar{Y} = b\bar{X} + a$$
Solving for this equation for the value of a yields,
$$a = \bar{Y} - b\bar{X}$$

4.   Remember that a regression equation should not be used to predict values outside the range of the original data.

SELF-TEST AND REVIEW

1.   A correlation measures the relationship between two variables, X and Y. The relationship may be described in terms of three characteristics: direction, form, and degree.

a.   How is the <u>direction</u> of relationship indicated in a correlation?

b.   How is the <u>degree</u>   (or magnitude) of a relationship indicated in a correlation?

c.   Describe what is mean by a "positive relationship."

d.   What is the "form" of relationship that is measured by the Pearson correlation?

2.   The formula for the Pearson correlation uses SP, or the Sum of Products, to measure how much X and Y vary together. When SP is large (either positive or negative) it indicates that there is a consistent relation between X and Y. However, when SP is near zero it indicates that there is no consistent relationship and X and Y tend to vary independently. Compute SP for the following sets of data. You should find that the definitional formula works well with Set I because both means are whole numbers. However, the computational formula is better with Set II where the means are fractions.

Data Set I	
X	Y
1	5
5	2
6	9
15	20
8	4

Data Set II	
X	Y
1	0
4	4
3	1
2	1

3.   The book identified three points of caution when you are working with correlations.

a. Describe the general problem associated with cause-and-effect relations.

b. Describe the general problem associated with restricted range.

c. If you obtain a correlation of r = 0.50, is it correct to view this correlation as being half-way between a perfect linear relation (1.00) and no relation (0.00)?

4. In the same way that a sample mean can be used to draw inferences about a population mean, you can use a sample correlation to draw inferences about the corresponding population correlation. The inferential procedure is a hypothesis test where the null hypothesis states that there is no relationship (zero correlation) between X and Y in the population. The test is conducted by simply comparing the sample correlation with a table of significant values. Suppose that a sample of n = 42 pairs of X and Y scores gives a Pearson correlation of r = +0.40. Does this sample provide sufficient evidence to conclude that a significant correlation exists in the population? Test at the .05 level of significance.

5. The general equation for expressing a linear relation between X and Y is

$\hat{Y} = bX + a$

a. In this equation, what name and interpretation is given to the value of b?

b. What name and interpretation is given to the value of a?

6. For the linear equation, Y = 2X + 6, find the value of Y that corresponds to each of the following X values.

X	Y
0	
1	
10	
-3	

7.   The regression equation for Y determines the best
fitting straight line for a set of X and Y data. This
equation is determined by minimizing the distance between
the actual Y values and the points on the line. The
regression equation is

$$\hat{Y} = bX + a$$

where $b = \dfrac{SP}{SS_X}$ and $a = \bar{Y} - b\bar{X}$

Find the regression equation for the following set
of data.

X	Y
4	1
7	16
3	4
5	7
6	7

8.   The regression equation can be used to compute a
predicted value of Y for any given value of X. The
distance or error between the predicted Y (on the line)
and the actual Y can be expressed as $(Y - \hat{Y})$. When these
error values are squared and summed, you obtain SS_{error}
for the regression equation. This SS value has df = n −
2 and can be used to compute a measure of accuracy of

prediction which is called the standard error of
estimate. In problem 7 you should have obtained the
regression equation, Y = 3X - 8. Using this equation and
the data from problem 7,

      a.   Compute the predicted Y value ($\hat{Y}$) for each X.

      b.   Compute the error, (Y - $\hat{Y}$) for each data point.

      c.   Compute SS_{error} for these data.

      d.   Compute the standard error of estimate.

9.   Rather than computing SS_{error} directly from the
error scores, this value can be found as a proportion of
SS_Y. Specifically,

$$SS_{error} = (1 - r^2)SS_Y$$

In this equation, the sample correlation, r, is used to
determine how much of the variability in Y is predicted
by regression and how much is unpredicted or "error"
variability. The predicted portion is determined by r^2
which is called the coefficient of determination. The
unpredicted, or error, portion is determined by $1 - r^2$.
Thus, the Y variability as measured by SS_Y can be
partitioned into two components,

$$SS_Y = SS_{predicted} + SS_{error}$$

$$1.00 = r^2 + (1 - r^2)$$

    a.   For the data in problem 7, $SS_Y = 126$. Compute
the Pearson correlation for these data.

    b.   Compute the coefficient of determination for
these data.

    c.   Multiply r^2 times SS_Y to obtain the predicted
portion of the Y variability.

d. Multiply $(1 - r^2)$ times SS_Y to obtain the error portion of the Y variability. (Note: This value is SS_{error}. You should obtain the same answer that you did in problem 8 where you calculated SS_{error} directly.)

10. For the following set of scores
   a. Compute the Pearson correlation.
   b. Find the regression equation for predicting Y from X.

X	Y
0	16
1	6
2	9
3	0
4	9

ANSWERS TO SELF-TEST

1. a. The direction of the relation is indicated by the sign (+ or -) of the correlation.
   b. The degree of relationship is indicated by the numerical value of the correlation. A value near 1 indicates a nearly perfect relation, and a value near 0 indicates no relationship.
   c. In a positive relationship both variables tend to change in the same direction: as X increases, Y also tends to increase.
   d. The Pearson correlation measures linear (straight line) relationships.
2. For data set I, SP = 121. For data set II, SP = 6.

3. a. A correlation between X and Y should not be

interpreted as a cause-effect relationship. Two variables can be related without one having a direct effect on the other.

b. With a restricted range you only see part of the relationship between X and Y. You should not generalize a correlation beyond the range of data for which it was obtained.

c. A correlation of 0.50 has a coefficient of determination of 0.25. The squared correlation gives a better indication of the value of the relationship for purposes of prediction.

4. The null hypothesis states that there is no relationship in the population.

H_0: $\rho = 0$

With n = 42, the correlation must be greater than 0.304 to be significant. This sample correlation is sufficient to conclude that there is a significant correlation in the population.

5. a. In the linear equation, b is called the slope constant. This value determines how much Y changes when X is increased by 1 point.

b. In the general linear equation, a is called the Y-intercept. This is the value of Y when X = 0, and it determines the point where the line crosses (intercepts) the Y-axis.

6.

X	Y
0	6
1	8
10	26
-3	0

7. For these data, $SS_X = 10$ and $SP = 30$. The regression equation is,

$$\hat{Y} = 3X - 8$$

8. a. The predicted Y values are in the third column of the following table.
    b. The error values are in the fourth column.

X	Y	$\hat{Y}$	$(Y - \hat{Y})$	$(Y - \hat{Y})^2$
4	1	4	-3	9
7	16	13	3	9
3	4	1	3	9
5	7	7	0	0
6	7	10	-3	9

    c. The squared error scores add to 36
    d. The standard error of estimate is $\sqrt{12} = 3.46$.

9. a. The Pearson correlation is r = 0.845.
    b. $r^2 = .714$.
    c. The predicted portion of SS_Y is 89.96.
    d. $(1 - r^2) = .286$ and the error portion of SS_Y is 36.04. Within rounding error, this is identical to the value of 36 you obtained for SS_{error} in problem 8c.

10. a. $SS_X = 10$, $SS_Y = 134$, and $SP = -20$. The Pearson correlation is r = -0.546.
    b. The regression equation is, $\hat{Y} = -2X + 12$.

CHAPTER 17 CHI SQUARE TESTS

LEARNING OBJECTIVES

1.   Recognize the experimental situations where a chi square tests is appropriate.

2.   Be able to conduct a chi square test for goodness of fit to evaluate a hypothesis about the shape of a population frequency distribution.

3.   Be able to conduct a chi square test for independence to evaluate a hypothesis about the relationship between two variables.

NEW TERMS AND CONCEPTS

The following terms were introduced in this chapter. Define or describe each term and, where appropriate, describe how each term is related to other terms in the list.

chi square test for goodness of fit
chi square test for independence
expected frequencies
observed frequencies

NEW FORMULAS

$$\chi^2 = \Sigma \frac{(f_o - f_e)^2}{f_e}$$

$$f_e = pn \quad \text{(for the goodness-of-fit test)}$$

$$f_e = \frac{(\text{row total})(\text{column total})}{n} \quad \text{(for the test of independence)}$$

STEP-BY-STEP

The chi square test for independence. The chi square test for independence uses frequency data to test a hypothesis about the relationship between two variables. The null hypothesis states that the two variables are independent (no relation). Rejecting H_0 indicates that the data provide convincing evidence of a consistent relation between the two variables. The following example will be used to demonstrate this chi square test.

A manufacturer of watches would like to examine preferences for digital versus analog watches. A sample of 200 people is obtained and these individuals are classified by age and preference. The manufacturer would like to know if there is a consistent relationship between age and preference. The frequency data are as follows:

		Digital	Analog	No Preference
Age	under 30	90	40	10
	over 30	10	40	10

Step 1: State the hypotheses and select an alpha level. The null hypothesis says that there is no relationship.

H_0: Preference is independent of age. In terms of frequencies, this hypothesis can be stated as, "the frequency distribution of preferences is the same for people under 30 as for people over 30."

The alternative hypothesis simply says that there is a relation.

H_1: Preference is related to age.

We will use $\alpha = .05$

Step 2: Locate the critical region. The degrees of freedom for the chi square test for independence are

$$df = (C - 1)(R - 1)$$

For this example, df = 2(1) = 2. Sketch the distribution
and locate the extreme 5%. The critical boundary is
5.99.

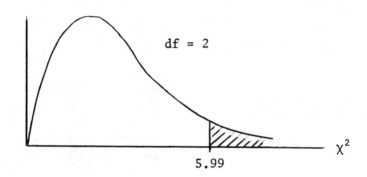

Step 3: Compute the test statistic. The major concern
for this chi square test is determining the expected
frequencies. We begin with a blank matrix showing only
the row and column totals from the data.

	Digital	Analog	No Preference	
Under 30				140
Over 30				60
	100	80	20	

The expected frequencies are determined by the null
hypothesis. In this example, H_0 says that the
distribution of preferences is the same for both age
groups. Therefore, we must determine the "distribution

of preferences." For this example of n = 200 we found

       100/200 = 50% prefer digital
        80/200 = 40% prefer analog
       20/200 = 10% have no preference

Next, we apply this distribution to each age group.
There are 140 individuals who are under 30. Using the
proportions we have found,
     50% of 140 = 70
     40% of 140 = 56
     10% of 140 = 14

For the group of 60 individuals who are over 30 years
old,

     50% of 60 = 30
     40% of 60 = 24
     10% of 60 =   6

Place these values in a matrix of expected frequencies.

	Digital	Analog	No Preference
under 30	70	56	14
over 30	30	24	6

Now you are ready to compute the chi square statistic.
    a) For each cell in the matrix, find the difference
between the expected and the observed frequency.
    b) Square the difference.
    c) Divide the squared difference by the expected
frequency.

f_o	f_e	$(f_o - f_e)$	$(f_o - f_e)^2$	$\dfrac{(f_o - f_e)^2}{f_e}$
90	70	20	400	5.71
40	56	16	256	4.57
10	14	4	16	1.14
10	30	20	400	13.33
40	24	16	256	10.67
10	6	4	16	2.67

Finally, add the values for each category.

$$\chi^2 = 38.09$$

Step 4: Make decision. The chi square value is in the critical region. Therefore, we reject H_0 and conclude that there is a significant relation between age and watch preference.

To describe the nature of the relationship, you can compare the data with the expected frequencies. From this comparison it should be clear that more younger people prefer digital watches and more older people prefer analog watches than would be expected by chance.

HINTS AND CAUTIONS

1. When computing expected frequencies for either chi square test, it is wise to check your arithmetic by being certain that $\Sigma f_e = \Sigma f_o = n$. In the test for independence, the expected frequencies in any row or

column should sum to the same total as the corresponding row or column in the observed frequencies.

2.   Whenever a chi square test has df = 1, the difference (absolute value) between f_e and f_o will be the same for every category. This is true for either the goodness of fit test with 2 categories, or the test of independence with 4 categories. Knowing this fact can help you check the calculation of expected frequencies and it can simplify the calculation of the chi square statistic.

SELF-TEST AND REVIEW

1.   The two chi square tests in this chapter are examples of what are called nonparametric tests. The t tests and ANOVA we considered earlier are all examples of parametric tests. Nonparametric tests differ from parametric tests in many ways.
     a. Explain how the data for a chi square test differ from the data for a t test or ANOVA.
     b. Explain how the assumptions for a chi square tests differ from the assumptions for a t test or ANOVA.
     c. Explain how the hypotheses for a chi square test differ from the hypotheses for a t test or ANOVA.

2.   The chi square test for goodness of fit evaluates a hypothesis about the shape of the population distribution. The null hypothesis specifies the proportion (or percentage) of the population in each category. These hypothesized proportions are then used to compute the expected frequencies for each category.

a. If H_0 predicts no preference among five brands of pizza, what would be the expected frequencies for a sample of n = 60 individuals?

b. If H_0 predicts that women outnumber men by 3 to 1 in the nursing profession, what would be the expected frequencies for a sample of n = 60 nurses? (Hint: a 3 to 1 ratio means that out of every four nurses, three are women and one is a man.)

3. The chi square statistic measures the discrepancy between the data (observed frequencies) and the hypothesis (expected frequencies) much the same as a t statistic.

a. What value of chi square tends to refute the null hypothesis: a large value or a small value? Explain your answer by referring to the structure of the chi square formula.

b. What is the meaning of a chi square square statistic of zero?

c. Can chi square ever be less than zero?

4. Like many other test statistics we have encountered, the chi square statistic has degrees of freedom. However, the chi square statistic is unique in that df for chi square is not related to the sample size (n). For the chi square test for goodness of fit,

a. What is the value of df for a test with four categories and a sample of n = 100?

b. What is the value of df for a test with four categories and a sample of n = 1000?

c. If a researcher reports a chi square statistic with df = 5, how many categories are in the distribution?

5.   The chi square test for independence is similar to a correlation in that it evaluates the relationship between two variables. The null hypothesis for the test of independence states that the two variables are independent. In terms of the sample data, describe the difference between a Pearson correlation and the chi square test for independence.

6.   The null hypothesis for the test of independence implies that the shape of the frequency distribution for one variable is the same for every category of the other variable. Thus, when the expected frequencies for this test are displayed in matrix, every row of the matrix will show the same set of proportions.
     a.   A researcher is testing four new flavors of bubblegum using a sample that consists of 50 men, 200 women, and 250 children. Each individual selects his/her favorite flavor. In the total sample of 500 people, 100 selected Flavor A, 200 chose B, 150 picked C, and only 50 preferred D. Use the matrix below to fill in the expected frequencies for a chi square test for independence.

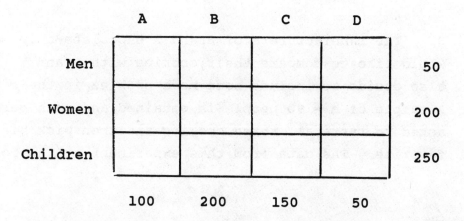

Flavor

	A	B	C	D	
Men					50
Women					200
Children					250
	100	200	150	50	

b.   Your expected frequencies should show ten out of
the fifty men in the sample, or p = 10/50 = .20, selected
Flavor A.   Compute the proportion of the men who select
each of the other flavors.   Next find the proportion of
the 200 women who selected each flavor.   Finally find the
four proportions for the 250 children.   Write your
proportions in the following matrix.   You should find
that every row has the same set of proportions.

Flavor

	A	B	C	D
Men	.20			
Women				
Children				

7.   The chi square test for independence also has
degrees of freedom that are determined by the number of
categories (not the sample size).   What would be the
value of df for the chi square test shown in problem #6?

8.   The manufacturers of Brand X chocolate-chip cookies
would like to compare their cookies with Brand Y.   They
also decide to include home-made cookies in their test.
A sample of n = 90 people is obtained and each person is
asked to taste all three cookies and then pick his/her
favorite.   The data from this experiment are as follows.

	Brand X	Brand Y	Home-Made
	21	18	51

Do these data indicate any significant preferences among the three types of cookies? Test at the .05 level of significance.

9.   Use the data from problem 8 to test the hypothesis that home-made cookies are preferred two-to-one over either brand. Test at the .05 level of significance.

10. A researcher is interested in the relationship between birth order and personality. A sample of n = 100 people is obtained, all of whom grew up in families as one of three children. Each person is given a personality test and the researcher also records the person's birth order position (1st born, 2nd, or 3rd). The frequencies from this study are shown in the following table. On the basis of these data can the researcher conclude that there is a significant relation between birth order and personality? Test at the .05 level of significance.

	Birth Position		
	1st	2nd	3rd
Outgoing	13	31	16
Reserved	17	19	4

1.   a.   The data for chi square tests consist of frequencies. For the parametric tests the data are scores that can be added, averaged, squared, etc..

     b.   The chi square tests make no assumptions about the populations from which data are obtained. The parametric tests, on the other hand, assume normal distributions and require homogeneity of variance for independent measures designs.

     c.   The chi square hypotheses refer to the entire population but do not mention any specific population parameters. In contrast, the parametric tests always test hypotheses about specific population parameters (generally the population means).

2.   a.   The expected frequency would be 12 for each of the five brands.

     b.   The expected frequencies are 45 women and 15 men for a sample of $n = 60$.

3.   a.   A large value for chi square tends to refute H_0. The chi square formula measures the difference between the expected and observed frequencies, so a large value indicates that the data do not fit the hypothesis.

     b.   A chi square value of zero indicates that there is a perfect fit between the data and the hypothesis.

     c.   The chi square statistic is computed by summing squared values. It can never be less than zero.

4.   a.   df = 3

     b.   df = 3   (The sample size does not influence df.)

     c.   There are six categories.

5.   For the chi square test, the individuals in the sample are simply classified and that data consist of frequencies. For a Pearson correlation, each individual is measured twice and the data consist of two scores for each individual.

6.   a. The expected frequencies are,

Flavor

	A	B	C	D
Men	10	20	15	5
Women	40	80	60	20
Children	50	100	75	25

b. You should obtain proportions of .20, .40, .30, and .10 for each row in the matrix.

7.   df = (C - 1)(R - 1) = 3(2) = 6

8.   The expected frequencies are 30, 30 and 30. For these data, χ^2 = 22.20. With df = 2, reject H_0 and conclude that there are significant preferences among the three types of cookies.

9.   The expected frequencies are 22.5, 22.5, and 45. For these data, χ^2 = 1.80. With df = 2, fail to reject H_0.

10.   The null hypothesis states that there is no relation between birth order and personality - the two variables

are independent. With df = 2, the critical value for
this test is 5.99. The expected frequencies are as
follows:

	1st born	2nd born	3rd born
Outgoing	18	30	12
Reserved	12	20	8

For these data, the chi square statistic is 6.89. Reject
H_0 and conclude that there is a significant relation
between personality and birth order.

CHAPTER 18

STATISTICAL METHODS FOR ORDINAL DATA

LEARNING OBJECTIVES

1. Know when the Mann-Whitney U and the Wilcoxon Signed-Ranks tests are appropriate.

2. Be able to compute and evaluate the Mann-Whitney U and the Wilcoxon T.

3. Understand the Spearman correlation and how it differs from the Pearson correlation in terms of the data it uses and the type of relationship it measures.

NEW TERMS AND CONCEPTS

The following terms were introduced in this chapter. Define or describe each term and, where appropriate, describe how each term is related to other terms in the list.

ordinal data
Mann-Whitney U
normal approximation to the Mann-Whitney U
Wilcoxon T
Spearman correlation
monotonic relation

NEW FORMULAS

$$U_A = n_A n_B + \frac{n_A(n_A + 1)}{2} - \Sigma R_A$$

$$U_B = n_A n_B + \frac{n_B(n_B + 1)}{2} - \Sigma R_B$$

$$U_A + U_B = n_A n_B$$

$$z = \frac{U - \frac{n_A n_B}{2}}{\sqrt{\frac{n_A n_B (n_A + n_B + 1)}{12}}} = \frac{U - \mu}{\sigma}$$

$$\text{where } \mu = \frac{n_A n_B}{2} \text{ and } \sigma = \sqrt{\frac{n_A n_B (n_A + n_B + 1)}{12}}$$

$$r_s = 1 - \frac{6 \Sigma D^2}{n(n^2 - 1)}$$

The Mann-Whitney U test: As a nonparametric alternative to the independent measures t, the Mann-Whitney test uses the data from two separate samples to test hypotheses about the difference between two populations or two treatments. The following example will be used to demonstrate the Mann-Whitney U test.

A researcher obtains two random samples with n = 5 in one sample and n = 6 in the other. Treatment A is administered to the first sample and the second sample gets Treatment B. The resulting scores for the two samples are:

    Sample A: 15, 12, 9, 19, 20
    Sample B: 8, 10, 5, 14,3, 6

Step 1: State the hypotheses and select an alpha level. The hypotheses for the Mann-Whitney U are stated in general terms and do not concern any specific population parameters.

    H_0: There is no systematic difference between the
            two treatments.

    H_1: There is a systematic difference that causes
            the scores from one sample to be generally
            higher than the scores from the other sample.

We will use α = .05.

Step 2: Locate the critical region. For the Mann-Whitney test, a small value of U indicates a substantial difference between the two samples. To determine the critical value, you must consult the Mann-Whitney table. With n = 5 and n = 6 for the two samples, and with α = .05, the critical value is U = 3. If the data produce U = 3 or smaller we will conclude that there is a significant difference between the two treatments.

Step 3: Compute the test statistic. Although the Mann-Whitney U does not require much calculation, there are several steps involved in finding the U value.

    a. Combine the two samples and list all the scores in rank-order from smallest to largest.

    b. For each individual in sample A, count how many of the scores from sample B have lower positions in the list. Sum these values for all the individuals in sample A. This is U_a.

    c. In the same way, find U_b.

    d. The Mann-Whitney U is the smaller of the two U values.

For these data:

Rank	1	2	3	4	5	6	7	8	9	10	11
Score	3	5	6	8	9	10	12	14	15	19	20
Sample	B	B	B	B	A	B	A	B	A	A	A
					:		:		:	:	:
Points for					:		:		:	:	:
Sample A					2		1		0	0	0

Sample A has a U value of U_a = 2 + 1 = 3
Using this same procedure, compute U for sample B. To check your calculations be sure that
$$U_a + U_b = n_a n_b$$
You should find that the smaller U is U = 3.

Make decision. The U value of U = 3 is in the critical region. This is a very unlikely value to obtain by chance, so we reject H_0 and conclude that there is a systematic difference between the two treatments.

The Wilcoxon test: As a nonparametric alternative to the repeated measures t, the Wilcoxon test uses data from a single sample measured in two treatment conditions. The difference scores for the sample are used to test a hypothesis about the difference between the treatments in the population. The following example will be used to demonstrate the Wilcoxon T test.

A researcher obtains a random sample of n = 7 individuals and tests each person in two different treatment conditions. The data for this sample are,

Subject	Treatment 1	Treatment 2	Difference
#1	8	24	+16
#2	12	10	- 2
#3	15	19	+ 4
#4	31	52	+21
#5	26	20	- 6
#6	32	40	+ 8
#7	19	29	+10

Step 1: State the hypotheses and select an alpha level. The hypotheses for the Wilcoxon test do not refer to any specific population parameter.

> H_0: There is no systematic difference between the
>   two treatments.

H_1: There is a consistent difference between the treatments that causes the scores in one treatment to be generally higher than the scores in the other treatment.

We will use $\alpha = .05$.

Step 2: Locate the critical region. A small value for the Wilcoxon T indicates that the difference scores were consistently positive (or consistently negative) which indicates a systematic treatment difference. Thus, small values will tend to refute H_0. To locate the critical value, consult the Wilcoxon table with n = 7 and $\alpha = .05$. For these data a Wilcoxon T of 2 or smaller is needed to reject H_0.

Step 3: Compute the test statistic. The calculation of the Wilcoxon T is very simple, but requires several stages.

    a. Ignoring the signs (+ or -), rank the difference scores from smallest to largest.

    b. Compute the sum of the ranks for the positive differences and the sum for the negative differences.

    c. The Wilcoxon T is the smaller of the two sums.

For these data,

Difference		Rank	
(+)	16	6	
(-)	2	1	
(+)	4	2	$\Sigma R_+ = 24$
(+)	21	7	
(-)	6	3	$\Sigma R_- = 4$
(+)	8	4	
(+)	10	5	

The Wilcoxon T is T = 4

Step 4: Make decision. The obtained T value is not in the critical region. These data are not significantly different from chance. Therefore, we fail to reject H_0 and conclude that there is not sufficient evidence to suggest a systematic difference between the two treatments.

Spearman Correlation: The Spearman correlation measures the degree of relationship between two variables that are both measured on ordinal scales. If the original data are from interval or ratio scales, you can first rank the scores, then compute the Spearman correlation. The following data will be used to demonstrate the calculation of the Spearman correlation.

X	Y	
5	12	
7	18	(Both X and Y are measured on
2	9	interval scales)
15	14	
10	13	

Step 1: Check that the X values and the Y values consist of ranks (ordinal data). If not, rank the Xs and rank the Ys. Caution: Rank X and Y separately.

For these data,

X Score	X Rank	Y Rank	Y Score
5	2	2	12
7	3	5	18
2	1	1	9
15	5	4	14
10	4	3	13

Step 2: To use the special Spearman formula, compute the difference (D) between the X rank and the Y rank for each individual. Also, find the squared difference (D^2) and the sum of the squared differences.

(Note: The signs of the difference scores are unimportant because you are squaring each D.)

X Rank	Y Rank	D	D^2
2	2	0	0
3	5	2	4
1	1	0	0
5	4	1	1
4	3	1	1

$$6 = \Sigma D^2$$

Step 3: Substitute D^2 and n in the Spearman formula.

$$r_s = 1 - \frac{6\Sigma D^2}{n(n^2 - 1)}$$

$$= 1 - \frac{6(6)}{5(24)}$$

$$= 1 - \frac{3}{10}$$

$$= 0.70$$

There is a positive relation between X and Y for these data. The correlation is fairly high (although not perfect) which indicates a very consistent positive relation.

HINTS AND CAUTIONS

1. Sometimes it is obvious from looking at the data which sample has the smaller Mann-Whitney U value. Nevertheless, it is wise to compute both U values and check your computations by the formula, $U_a + U_b = n_a n_b$.

2. Remember, to be significant the Mann-Whitney U and the Wilcoxon T must be <u>equal to or less than</u> the critical value provided in the table.

3. In computing the Wilcoxon T, it is important to remember that these signs should be ignored when ranking the difference scores.

4. The special formula for the Spearman correlation often causes trouble. Remember, the value of the fraction is computed separately and then subtracted from 1.00. The 1 is not a part of the fraction.

SELF-TEST AND REVIEW

1. All of the nonparametric procedures in this chapter require that the data be rank-ordered. Often the process

of ranking requires that tied scores be ranked.
Demonstrate this process by ranking the following scores:
    Scores: 3, 8, 8, 10, 14, 14, 14, 27, 35, 100

2.   The Mann-Whitney test is a nonparametric alternative
to the independent measures t test.   However, the Mann-
Whitney test does not require normal distributions or
homogeneity of variance, and the data for the Mann-
Whitney test only need to be measured on an ordinal
scale.   State the null hypothesis for the Mann-Whitney
test and explain how it differs from H_0 for the
independent measures t test.

3.   To obtain the test statistic U for the Mann-Whitney
test, the scores from the two samples are combined in a
single list and then ranked.   The U value is determined
by a counting procedure or by a formula using the sum of
the ranks for each sample.
    a.   Compute the Mann-Whitney U for the following
data.

Sample 1	Sample 2
3	12
5	8
7	15
4	9
3	6
10	9

    b.   In the following data, two samples (A and B) have
been combined and rank-ordered.   Find the U value for
each of the two samples.

Rank	Sample
1	A
2	A
3	B
4	A
5	B
6	A
7	A
8	B
9	B
10	A

4.   The null hypothesis is rejected in a Mann-Whitney test if the obtained U value is less than or equal to the critical value in the table. Explain why a <u>small</u> U value is an indication of a consistent difference between the two treatments.

5.   The table of critical values for the Mann-Whitney test does not cover situations where the sample sizes are greater than n = 20. Briefly explain how the Mann-Whitney test is conducted with n > 20.

6.   A psychologist performs a study to assess the effect of meaning on memory. One sample of subjects is asked to study a list of nonsense syllables (such as LIF) that have no meaning. A second group studies a similar list and these subjects are told to try to remember the syllables by thinking of something to give it meaning (imagine a person laughing for LAF). Later in the experiment, subjects are given a recognition test. They are presented with a long list of syllables and must indicate those which were on the original list that they studied. The psychologist records the number of items

recognized. For the data below, determine if the treatments are significantly different. Use the Mann-Whitney test and α = .05.

Sample A Low Meaning	Sample B High Meaning
14	25
6	23
9	19
27	29
16	30
22	24
7	21

7. The Wilcoxon test is a nonparametric alternative to the repeated measures t test. Each individual in a sample is measured in two treatment conditions, and a difference score is obtained. To compute the Wilcoxon T statistic, the difference scores must be ranked without regard to their signs.

   a. Rank the following difference scores and find the Wilcoxon T for this sample.

   Difference Scores: -8, 2, -10, -4, 7, -13, -17, -9

   b. Occasionally it is necessary to rank tied scores. Find the Wilcoxon T for the following sample.

   Difference Scores: 4, -3, -11, -4, 8, -12, -3, -15

8. Briefly explain the two methods for handling difference scores of zero for the Wilcoxon T.

9. A psychologist would like to assess the effect of peer group support on weight reduction. A group of 10 people meet weekly to discuss weight loss and provide emotional and motivational support for one another.

After six weeks, the psychologist records their weights to get a preliminary assessment of the effectiveness of the program. Use the Wilcoxon test to determine if a significant change has occurred after just six weeks. Set alpha at .05. The weights before the experiment and after six weeks of meetings are as follows:

Subject	Before	After
A	201	195
B	158	150
C	151	141
D	150	143
E	171	172
F	146	149
G	162	171
H	147	142
I	145	134
J	150	138

10. The Spearman correlation measures the relationship between two variables measured on ordinal scales. As with the Pearson correlation, Spearman can be either positive or negative, and its magnitude ranges from 0 (no relation) to 1.00 (a perfectly consistent relation). Occasionally a researcher will use the Spearman correlation with data that are measured on an interval or ratio scale.

a. Explain how the Spearman correlation is calculated with data from an interval or ratio scale.

b. Explain what information is provided by the Spearman correlation when the data are from interval or ratio scales.

11. Compute the Spearman correlation for each of the following sets of data.

Set 1		Set 2	
X and Y measured on ordinal scales		X and Y measured on interval scales	
X	Y	X	Y
2	5	1	5
4	1	5	2
3	2	6	9
1	4	15	20
5	3	8	4

ANSWERS TO SELF-TEST

1. When two scores are tied, their ranks should also be tied.

Scores:	3	8	8	10	14	14	14	27	35	100
Ranks:	1	2.5	2.5	4	6	6	6	8	9	10

2. The null hypothesis for the Mann-Whitney test simply states that there is no systematic difference between the two treatments (or populations) being compared. The hypothesis does not mention any specific population parameters. On the other hand, the independent measures t test evaluates hypotheses about the two population means.

3. a. When the two samples are combined and listed in order the result is as follows:

Score	Sample	Rank	Points for #2
3	#1	1.5	
3	#1	1.5	
4	#1	3	
5	#1	4	
6	#2	5	----------- 2
7	#1	6	
8	#2	7	----------- 1
9	#2	8.5	----------- 1
9	#2	8.5	----------- 1
10	#1	10	
12	#2	11	----------- 0
15	#2	12	----------- 0

Sample #2 has a total of U = 5 points. By a similar calculation, you should find that Sample #1 has a total of U = 31 points. The Mann-Whitney U is the smaller value, so U = 5.

b. Because sample B appears to be at the bottom of the ranking, this sample should have the smaller U value. The calculation of the points for sample B is shown below:

Rank	Sample	Points for B
1	A	
2	A	
3	B	--------- 4
4	A	
5	B	--------- 3
6	A	
7	A	
8	B	--------- 1
9	B	--------- 1
10	A	

Thus, sample B has a total of 9 points. You should find that sample A has 15 points.

4. A small U value indicates that one of the two samples has a small point total. This means that one sample has scored consistently higher than the other so that the two samples are clustered at opposite ends of the ranking. When this occurs, it indicates a consistent and systematic difference between the two treatments being compared.

5. When the samples are large, the Mann-Whitney U tends to form a normal distribution. In this case you can compute a z-score for any U value, and then consult the unit normal table to determine whether or not the U value is significant.

6. For sample A, U = 7, and for sample B, U = 42. The Mann-Whitney U is 7 which is in the critical region. Reject the null hypothesis and conclude that meaningfulness does affect memory.

7. a. When the difference scores are ranked in order of magnitude, it is clear that the positive values have the smaller sum of ranks.

Difference	Rank	
2	1	
-4	2	The positive differences
7	3	have ranks of 1 and 3,
-8	4	so T = 1 + 3 = 4
-9	5	
-10	6	
-13	7	
-17	8	

b. Begin by ranking the scores without regard to sign.

Difference	Rank	
-3	1.5	
-3	1.5	The positive differences
4	3.5	have ranks of 3.5 and 5,
-4	3.5	so T = 3.5 + 5 = 8.5.
8	5	
-11	6	
-12	7	
-15	8	

8.   There are two methods of dealing with difference scores of zero in a Wilcoxon test. First, you can discard the zeros and reduce the sample size. This method ignores the fact that zero differences tend to support the null hypothesis. Because it throws out data that support H_0, the practice of discarding zeros can increase the chances that you will reject the null hypothesis and increase the risk of a Type I error. The second method involves dividing the zero differences equally among the positive and negative values and ranking the zeros along with the other scores.

9.   The null hypothesis states that the weight reduction program has no systematic effect on weight. For these data the positive differences have ranks of 1, 2, and 7. The Wilcoxon T = 10. This value is not in the critical region for n = 10, so we fail to reject the null hypothesis.

10.   a.   If you begin with data from an interval or ratio
scale, the fist step is to rank the X values and then
rank the Y values. Remember, X and Y are ranked
separately. Then compute the Spearman correlation using
the ranks.

      b.   With interval or ratio scale data, the Spearman
correlation measures the consistency of direction of the
relationship without regard to the form of the relation.

11.   For data set 1, the Spearman correlation is
$r_s = -0.60$.   After ranking the scores in data
set 2, the Spearman correlation is $r_s = +0.50$.

• • • INTRODUCTION TO MINITAB • • •

1. GETTING STARTED
A Simple Example

To help acquaint you with Minitab, we'll start by showing
you a simple Minitab session. Text typed by the user is
underlined. Text typed by the computer is not.

```
MTB >  Retrieve 'Trees'
MTB >  INFO

Column      Name         Count
  C1        Diameter       31
  C2        Height         31
  C3        Volume         31

Constants used: none
MTB >  Describe C1 C2 C3
              N      MEAN     MEDIAN     TRMEAN     STDEV     SEMEAN
DIAMETER 31   13.248   12.900     13.156     3.138     0.564
HEIGHT   31   76.00    76.00      76.15      6.37      1.14
VOLUME   31   30.17    24.20      28.87      16.44     2.95

              MIN      MAX        Q1          Q3
DIAMETER  8.300   20.600     11.000      16.000
HEIGHT    63.00   87.00      72.00       80.00
VOLUME    10.20   77.00      19.10       38.30

MTB >  CORRELATION OF 'HEIGHT' vs 'VOLUME'
Correlation of HEIGHT and VOLUME = 0.598

MTB >  LET C4 = 'HEIGHT'/'VOLUME'
MTB >  NAME C4 'DENSITY'
MTB >  HISTOGRAM C4

Histogram of Density  N = 31
Midpoint Count
     1.0        1 *
     1.5        5 *****
     2.0        3 ***
     2.5        4 ****
     3.0        3 ***
     3.5        5 *****
     4.0        5 *****
     4.5        2 **
     5.0        0
     5.5        0
     6.0        1 *
     6.5        1 *
     7.0        1 *
```

Minitab - page 236

The data set used in the example consists of measurements collected from black cherry trees from Allegheny National Forest, Pennsylvania. As the above illustration shows, with just seven simple commands you can instruct Minitab to input data, check the status of the Minitab worksheet, calculate descriptive statistics for three variables, determine how highly correlated two variables are, create a new variable, name it and graphically depict its contents.

AN OVERVIEW

Minitab consists of a worksheet plus commands. The worksheet is where you keep your data while you're running Minitab, and commands are how you operate on that data while it's there.

The worksheet consists of columns plus constants. A column is designed to hold a series of numbers - like the heights of 31 black cherry trees, while a constant holds just one number - like the average height of the trees. In general, columns correspond to variables, and each row of a column corresponds to a single observation.

The Minitab worksheet is a temporary storage area for your data. Whenever you begin a Minitab session, a new worksheet is created. Until you enter numbers into the worksheet, it is empty and looks something like this:

```
        C1      C2      C3     . . . . . . . . . . . .
   1 |_____|_____|_____|_____
   2 |_____|_____|_____|_____
   3 |_____|_____|_____|_____
   4 |_____|_____|_____|_____
   5 |_____|_____|_____|_____
   . |_____|_____|_____|_____
   . |_____|_____|_____|_____

      K1 [ ]     K2 [ ]     K3 [ ] . . . . . . . .
```

In the above illustration, C1 stands for the first column in the worksheet, C2 for the second column, and so on. Likewise, K1 denotes the first constant, K2 the second, and so on.

Whenever you end a Minitab session, the worksheet and any data in it disappear. Therefore, if you have important data in the worksheet, save it in a file before exiting Minitab. (Section 2 explains how to do this.)

You instruct Minitab to do things by typing in commands. Most Minitab commands consist of a command name followed by argument.

Minitab will recognize approximately 180 command names, most of which are simple English words like TABLE, PLOT, and TALLY. Arguments can be numbers, columns, constants, or filenames. The first line of our opening example shows a command name, RETRIEVE, followed by a single argument, a file named TREES.

There are several shortcuts for entering commands. You can abbreviate command names by typing only their first four letters. You can add or delete text between command names and arguments as you see fit. You can refer to columns by name or by number. (See Section 3 for an explanation of naming columns). Finally, you can abbreviate series of consecutive column numbers by using a hyphen. As a result, the third and fourth commands in our opening example could have been shortened to:

```
MTB > DESC C1-C3
MTB > CORR C2   C3
```

Some Minitab commands can be followed by one or more subcommands. To tell Minitab that subcommands are to follow, end your command line with a semicolon. Minitab will respond with a different prompt, SUBC>. Each subcommand must be placed on a separate line, and all but the final subcommand in a series must end with a semicolon. The final subcommand must end with a period.

To start Minitab on most computers, type: MINITAB .
Minitab will respond with a few introductory remarks and then the Minitab prompt: MTB>. Minitab will then wait for you to begin entering commands.

When you want to end your Minitab session, type STOP.

HELP

Minitab provides a very complete HELP facility that you can access at any time. To learn how to use HELP, type HELP HELP. To see what commands Minitab has, type HELP COMMANDS. For help on a specific command, for example, HISTOGRAM, type HELP HISTOGRAM.

2.   ENTERING DATA

The first thing you'll want to do in any Minitab session is
enter data into the Minitab worksheet. You can enter data
from the keyboard, from a data file, or from a saved Minitab
worksheet.

From the Keyboard

SET puts all the numbers you type into one column. For
example, to enter numbers into C1, type

        MTB > SET C1

Minitab will respond with a different prompt, DATA >, and then
wait for you to type in number. Type:

        DATA > 2 4 6.5 0.2

Minitab will place all of those numbers into C1 and once again
respond with DATA >.   Type:

        DATA > 10 -0.1 14

Tell Minitab that you've finished entering data by typing:

Data > END

Minitab then returns you to the MTB > prompt.

READ enters data into several columns at once. For example,
to enter data into C2, C3, and C4, type:

        MTB > READ C2-C4
        DATA > 1 2 3
        DATA > 4 5 6
        DATA > 7 8 9
        DATA > 10 11 12
        DATA > END

Now let's take a look at all the data we've just entered.
Type:

        MTB > PRINT C1 - C4

Minitab displays your data like this:

ROW	C1	C2	C3	C4
1	2	1	2	3
2	4	4	5	6
3	6.5	7	8	9
4	0.2	10	11	12
5	10			
6	- 0.1			
7	14			

From a Data File

Quite often your data already reside on a file on your
computer. If your data file is a standard text (or ASCII)
file, you can input its contents directly into the Minitab
worksheet.

When all the data in your file are observations of a single
variable, you'll want to put them into a single column of the
worksheet. To illustrate how this is done, we'll use an
imaginary file. called EXAMPLE, that contains the following
data.

```
11    22    33
44    55    66
77    88    99
```

To place all nine numbers into C5, type:

MTB > <u>SET 'EXAMPLE' C5</u>

C5 then contains 11, 22, 33, 44, 55, 66, 77, 88, 99.

As you can see, Minitab reads a data file one row at a time
from left to right.

If your data file contains observations from several different
variables (one observation of each variable on each line), use
the command READ. For example, to input the data from our
EXAMPLE file into C6, C7,and C8 type READ 'EXAMPLE' C6-C7.

From a Saved Minitab Worksheet

It is important to distinguish between the Minitab worksheet and a *saved* Minitab worksheet. The Minitab worksheet provides temporary storage for your data; it appears when you begin your Minitab session and disappears when you end it. During your session, however, you can permanently store your data in a saved Minitab worksheet on a disk. Saved worksheets are special (binary) files that only Minitab can access, that are very fast to store and retrieve, and that contain both numbers and column names.

It is also important to distinguish between data files, which were discussed in the preceding section, and saved worksheets. Data files are stored in standard (ASCII) format that other software programs, such as data editors, can access, and can be transferred from computer to computer. The commands READ, WRITE, SET, and INSERT are used with data files; SAVE and RETRIEVE are used with saved Minitab worksheets.

To illustrate the use of saved worksheets, we'll use the TREES worksheet that is provided with every copy of Minitab. To copy the contents of the saved worksheet, TREES, into the Minitab worksheet, type:

        MTB > <u>RETRIEVE 'TREES'</u>

Note: If the TREES worksheet is not located in your current directly, Minitab will respond with an error and tell you that the requested file does not exist. In that case, you'll have to supply a pathname that tells Minitab where to find it. On microcomputers running MS-DOS, for example, you might type something like:

        RETRIEVE 'C:\MINITAB\HANDBOOK\TREES'

Minitab fetches TREES, inputs its contents into the Minitab worksheet, and responds with MTB>. Whenever you enter a RETRIEVE command, any data that is in the worksheet at the time will disappear.

3. SOME USEFUL COMMANDS

Checking the Worksheet Status

What does your worksheet look like now that you've retrieved
TREES? The easiest way to check the status of your worksheet
is to type:

```
MTB >  INFO

COLUMN       NAME        COUNT
C1           DIAMETER      31
C2           HEIGHT        31
C3           VOLUME        31

CONSTANTS USED: NONE
```

As you can see, INFO lists all of the columns and constants
that contain data, column names (when applicable), and the
total number of values in each column.

The data in TREES will be used in all subsequent examples. A
sample of black cherry trees in the Allegheny National Forest
of Pennsylvania were cut, and the diameter, height, and
volume were recorded in the corresponding columns. (The
forestry industry uses this type of information to estimate
the amount of available timber in a specific area.) (The data
were obtained from: H. Arthur Meyer, Forest Mensuration.
1953. Penns Valley Publishers, Inc., State College, PA.)

Naming Variables

Preceding sections have demonstrated the use of named columns;
this section explains how and why to name your columns. Quite
simply, naming columns makes your variables much easier to
reference and your output easier to read. The following
command was used to name C1 through C3 of TREES:

```
MTB >  NAME C1 'DIAMETER' C2 'HEIGHT' C3 'VOLUME'
```

You can name one or several columns with a single NAME
command. The names you choose may be from one to eight
characters in length, cannot include an apostrophe (or single
quote), and cannot begin or end with a blank. Once you've
named a variable, you may refer to it by its name or by its
number, as the following example illustrates:

MTB> <u>READ C1 'HEIGHT'</u>

Whenever you refer to a variable name, you must enclose the
name in single quotes. To change the name of a variable, just
issue another NAME command for that column.

Viewing Data

You can view data in your worksheet at any time using the
PRINT command. For example, to view the contents of C1 and
C2, type:

MTB> <u>PRINT C1 C2</u>

ROW	DIAMETER	HEIGHT
1	8.3	70
2	8.6	65
3	8.8	63
4	10.5	72
5	10.7	81
6	10.8	83
7	11.0	66
8	11.0	75
9	11.1	80
10	11.2	75
11	11.3	79
12	11.4	76
13	11.4	76
14	11.7	69
15	12.0	75
16	12.9	74
17	12.9	85
18	13.3	86
19	13.7	71
20	13.8	64

CONTINUE? <u>N</u>

When the columns you're printing contain more data than will fit on a single screen, Minitab will display one screen at a time, and after each one it will ask you if you wish to continue. To conserve space, we ended the above example after one screen of data by typing N after CONTINUE?. You may, of course, respond with Y to view additional data.

Correcting Errors in Data

You can use the LET command to assign a new value to an incorrect value. Suppose the sixteenth value in C1 should have been 12.7 instead of 12.9. You would change that value by typing:

MTB >   LET C1 (16) = 12.7

You have now assigned a new value, 12.7, to the 16th observation of C1. Since you can always substitute a column name for a column number you could have typed:

MTB>   LET 'DIAMETER'(16)=12.7

Note, however, that the row number must always be enclosed in parentheses.

Two other commands, INSERT and DELETE help you correct the worksheet. Type HELP INSERT and HELP DELETE to learn about them.

Arithmetic Transformations

The LET command in our opening example created a new variable equal to a tree's height divided by its volume and it is an example of an arithmetic transformation. Algebraic expressions used in a LET commend (e.g., C4 = 'HEIGHT'/'VOLUME') may contain the following operators:

+ for addition   / for division
- for subtraction   ** for exponentiation (raise to
* for multiplication   a power)

Minitab - page 244

In addition, LET commands may contain functions such as square
root, logarithm, absolute value, and many others. When using
statistical functions that yield a single number, you may
assign the result of a LET command to a constant. A few
examples using functions and constants follow:

```
MTB >   LET K1=MEAN(C1)
MTB >   LET K2=STDEV(C2)
MTB >   LET K3-MEDIAN('HEIGHT')
MTB >   PRINT K1-K3
K1      13.2484
K2      6.37181
K3      76.0000
```

4.   PLOTTING

Minitab permits you to depict your data graphically in various
histograms and scatterplots. Some plots summarize your data,
others depict patterns in your data over time, and still
others illustrate the relationship between two variables.
We'll illustrate just a few of them in this section.

Several plots summarize your data into a frequency
distribution. Our opening example presented one such display,
a histogram, and the following example presents a similar
display, a dotplot. Type:

```
MTB>   DOTPLOT 'DIAMETER'
                  .
        ....        .    .                                    .
  ...   ......     ..  ....       ..      ..  .        .
+---------+---------+---------+---------+--------+---------+
7.50     10.00     12.50     15.00     17.50    20.00  DIAMETER
```

This dotplot shows the distribution of the data contained in
DIAMETER, where each dot represents one datum point. As the
above example indicates, Minitab automatically chooses "nice"
scales for all plots, unless you specify your own.

There are several plots that depict the relationship between
two variables. One is a simple two-dimensional scatterplot.
Type:

MTB > PLOT'VOLUME''HEIGHT'

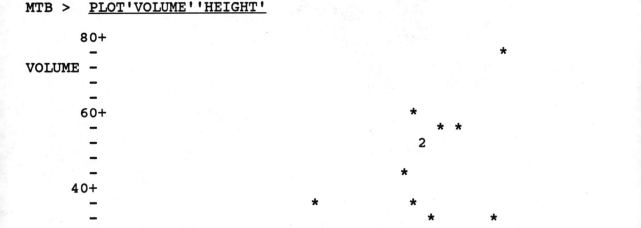

Here, an asterisk is displayed for each observation. When
several points are clustered close together, the total number
of points in the cluster is displayed instead of an asterick
(up to a total of 9; A "+" sign is used to represent 10 or
more data points). Notice that the variable listed first in
the commands is plotted on the y axis (i.e., the vertical
axis), and the second variable is plotted on the X axis (i.e.,
horizontal axis).

5.   STATISTICS: SOME SIMPLE EXAMPLES

Minitab can perform a wide variety of statistical analyses.
Here we will illustrate some typical ones. The following
examples use the TREES data set described in Section 3.

DESCRIBE

Our opening example illustrates the use of the DESCRIBE
command to produce descriptive statistics. To obtain these
for DIAMETER, type:

```
    MTB > DESCRIBE 'DIAMETER'

                N       MEAN     MEDIAN    TRMEAN    STDEV    SEMEAN
    DIAMETER   31      13.248    12.900    13.156    3.138    0.564

               MIN       MAX        Q1        Q3
    DIAMETER  8.300    20.600    11.000    16.000
```

As you can see, DESCRIBE provides you with: counts, means,
medians, 5% trimmed means, standard deviations, standard
errors of the mean, minimum and maximum values, and the first
and third quartiles.

T TEST

Suppose you want to test a claim that the average height of
black cherry trees is 72 feet. Type:

```
    MTB > TTEST 72'HEIGHT'
    TEST OF MU = 72.00 VS MU N.E. 72.00

               N       MEAN    STDEV    SEMEAN      T    P VALUE
    HEIGHT    31      76.00     6.37     1.14     3.50   0.0015
```

The TTEST command performs a two-sided t-test on the data in
HEIGHT. The small p-value (or significance level) of .0015
indicates that the average height is not equal to 72.

REGRESSION

In Section 4, we graphically depicted the relationship between
VOLUME and HEIGHT with a scatterplot. Now let's formulate an
equation that describes this relationship in greater detail.
Type:

    MTB > REGRESS 'VOLUME' ON 1 PREDICTOR 'HEIGHT'

or more simply:

    MTB > REGRESS 'VOLUME' 1 'HEIGHT'

    The regression equation is
    WEIGHT = -87.1 + 1.54 HEIGHT

Predictor	Coef	Stdev	t-ratio
Constant	-87.12	29.27	-2.98
HEIGHT	1.5433	0.3839	4.02

    s = 13.40   R-sq = 35.8%   R-sq(adj) = 33.6%

    Analysis of Variance

SOURCE	DF	SS	MS
Regression	1	2901.2	2901.2
Error	29	5204.9	179.5
Total	30	8106.1	

    Unusual Observations

obs.	HEIGHT	VOLUME	Fit	Stdev.Fit	Residual	St.Resid
31	87.0	77.00	47.15	4.86	29.85	2.39R

    R denotes an obs. with a large st. resid.

From REGRESS we have obtained the linear regression equation
as well as a great deal of additional information.

 Minitab - page 248

6.   OUTPUT

As you worked through all of the above examples, your results were displayed on the screen before you. You can also produce a permanent record of your results either on paper or in a file.

Storing Results on Paper

To produce a written record of your results, you'd type:

        MTB > PAPER

All of the commands you type after PAPER, as well as the results of those commands, will be sent to a printer and to your screen simultaneously. (On some computers, output is sent to a temporary print file instead of directly to a printer.) When you exit Minitab, this file is automatically printed and then disappears.

To produce a page advance (form feed) on your printer, you'd type:

        MTB > NEWPAGE

You can stop sending output to a printer at any time by typing:

        MTB > NOPAPER

During a single Minitab session you can start and stop sending output to a printer as many times as you wish.

Storing Results in a File

If you want to save your results for later use, or if you want
to edit your results, you can store them in a permanent file.
To send your output to a file called RESULTS, you'd type:

        MTB > <u>OUTFILE 'RESULTS'</u>

Now, all output (your commands and Minitab's results) will be
sent to the RESULTS file and to your screen simultaneously.
To stop sending output to RESULTS, type:

        MTB > <u>NOOUTFILE</u>

As with PAPER, you can turn OUTFILE "on" and "off" as many
times as you like in a single session. If you use OUTFILE
with the same filename several times, all of the output will
appear in a specific file, i.e., OUTFILE appends. In
addition, you can send output to several different files
during the same session.

Storing Data in a Saved Worksheet

If you have important data in your worksheet, store it in a
saved worksheet before you exit Minitab. Also, it is a good
idea to save your data from time to time as you work. This is
insurance against any errors you may make while manipulating
your data (like erasing the wrong column). The quickest and
easiest way to save your data is to store it in a saved
Minitab worksheet. A saved worksheet is a "snapshot" of the
Minitab worksheet at a particular moment in time. When you
type:

        MTB > <u>SAVE 'WSHEET'</u>

all the data in the Minitab worksheet at that time, as well as
all column names, are placed in a saved worksheet called
WSHEET. If you RETRIEVE the WSHEET file data during a
subsequent Minitab session, the Minitab worksheet will become
exactly the same as it was at the moment you saved WSHEET.

Minitab - page 250

Storing Data in a Data File

You can also store some or all of your data in a standard data (ASCII) file that other software programs can read. Type:

        MTB > <u>WRITE 'DATFIL' C1-C2</u>

Minitab creates a file called DATFIL and places the contents of C1 and C2 in it.

The contents of any file that you create with WRITE can be entered into Minitab using READ, SET, or INSERT.

• • • INTRODUCTION TO SPSS–X • • •

A
SAMPLE
SPSS-X
JOB

SPSS-X(tm) and SPSS/PC+(tm) commands are quite similar but not entirely identical. The following job is written for SPSS-X but requires little modification to run under SPSS/PC+.

An SPSS-X job consists of a number of commands, from a few to many hundreds, arranged in a logical order to carry out a set of functions. Figure 1 illustrates a typical sequence of commands. You could enter these commands interactively one at a time or place them all in a file and enter them all at once in a batch job. The mode of entering the commands is not important. What is important is how the commands fit together to carry out the desired job. The commands fall into three main steps:

⊕ Bring in some data to create an active file. If the data come from anything other than an SPSS-X system file or one of the other self-defining files that SPSS-X reads, the specifications will have to include names for the variables to be read and the way the values for each variable are recorded in the file.

⊕ Perform any transformations necessary to get the data in shape for analysis. This may involve changing the coding system or creating a new variable based on the values of existing variables.

⊕ Perform one of the procedures that list, tabulate, or analyze the data in the active file.

Sample job

Each of these steps can be repeated any number of times. To
minimize processing time, SPSS-X doesn't actually read the
data and create the active file or perform transformations
until it needs the data to carry out a procedure. Then it
performs all of those operations at once.

     In the job in Figure 1, a small amount of data is
defined, entered along with the SPSS-X commands, and then used
to update an older file of information about the employment
history of a middle-sized company. The variable of interest,
average salary increase, isn't included in this file, but it
is easily created using beginning and current salaries and the
date each employee joined the firm. A listing of a few cases
is requested as a way of making sure that the transformation
specifications are correct, and then several quick analyses
provide further understanding of the data.

Figure 1   Input for an SPSS-X Job

```
file handle empdatal /name = 'empdatal spssxfil *'
file handle empdata2 /name = 'empdata2 spssxfil a'

SET WIDTH 80 MXWARNS 200

DATA LIST FREE / ID SALNOW

BEGIN DATA
629 12800
886 7150
962 12667
1112 14300
1129 9600
END DATA

UPDATE FILE=EMPDATA1 / FILE=* / BY ID / MAP

COMPUTE AVGRAISE = (SALNOW-SALBEG)
                 /TRUNC(CTIME.DAYS($TIME-BEGDATE)/365.25)
VARIABLE LABELS  AVGRAISE 'AVERAGE ANNUAL RAISE'
PRINT FORMATS  AVGRAISE  (DOLLAR9.2)

LIST VARIABLES = ID BEGDATE SALNOW AVGRAISE
    /CASES = FROM 1 TO 50 BY 5

FREQUENCIES  VARIABLES = ALL
    /FORMAT = LIMIT(8) /HBAR  /STATISTICS

CROSSTABS  TABLES = MINORITY BY SEX  /STATISTICS

MEANS  TABLES = AVGRAISE BY MINORITY BY SEX

ANOVA  VARIABLES = AVGRAISE BY MINORITY (0,1) SEX (0,1)

PLOT  FORMAT = REGRESSION
    /PLOT = SALNOW WITH SALBEG BY SEX
```

Sample job

SET sets a maximum width of 80 columns for the display file. Width is one of many parameters that can be set to control the appearance of the output and other functions within SPSS-X operations.

DATA LIST describes the new data enclosed between the BEGIN DATA and END DATA commands. The data are in freefield format (with blanks separating values) and contain the two variables ID and SALNOW. These data represent salary adjustments made since the last update of the employee file. Once defined, these variables constitute the SPSS-X active file.

UPDATE brings in a previously saved SPSS-X system file, EMPDATA1, and uses the current active file (represented as *) to update the salary variable. The cases in the two files are matched by the variable ID. Where the IDs match, the new value for SALNOW replaced the value on EMPDATA1. The MAP subcommand asks for a record of the variables involved in the updating process. The output is in Figure 2.

COMPUTE creates a new variable, AVGRAISE, the average annual raise. To do this, we subtract beginning salary (SALBEG) from current salary (SALNOW) and divide this number by the number of complete years the employee has worked for the company. To get the number of years, we subtract the beginning date (BEGDATE) from the current date ($TIME, a value supplied by SPSS-X), convert that number to days (the CTIME.DAYS function), divide by 365.25, and finally truncate it to an integer.

Truncating years in this computation assumes that raises are given at the end of each year of service. For employees with less than a year's service, this function results in an arithmetically impossible division by zero. In this case, SPSS-X issues a warning and assigns a system-missing value, which causes the individual to be excluded from the analysis of average salary increase.

VARIABLE LABELS supplies the label "AVERAGE ANNUAL RAISE" for AVGRAISE. This label will be used in output from SPSS-X procedures.

PRINT FORMATS specifies that AVGRAISE be printed in dollar format (with a dollar sign and commas) in a nine-character field including two decimal places.

LIST simply lists the values of specified variables for the specified cases. See the output in Figure 3.

FREQUENCIES produces frequency tables, bar charts, histograms, and descriptive statistics. The specifications here request frequency tables only for variables with 8 or fewer categories. The HBAR subcommand requests histograms for variables with many values and bar carts for variables with fewer variables. Note in Figures 4 and 5 that FREQUENCIES produces a table, bar chart, and statistics for minority classification (which has two values) and a histogram and statistics for current salary (which has many values). The STATISTICS subcommand requests just the default statistics; many more descriptive statistics are available.

CROSSTABS produces the crosstabulation or contingency table in Figure 6. The chi-square statistic indicates no significant relationship between sex and minority classification. Again, many other statistics are available.

MEANS provides means and other descriptive statistics for AVGRAISE within subgroups defined by the categories of MINORITY and SEX within MINORITY. The table of means is in Figure 7. The obvious disparity in mean salary between mean and women and between white and nonwhite employees invites further investigations.

ANOVA produces the analysis of variance in Figure 8. This analysis shows a highly significant difference in average salary increase between minority groups (less than .05 percent chance that the difference occurs by chance) and a somewhat less strong difference between sexes (2.9 percent chance that the difference occurs by chance). The interaction effect, however, is not significant.

PLOT provides a visual representation of the relationship between current salary (SALNOW) and beginning salary (SALBEG). This specification requests a control variable, SEX, which causes individual points on the plot to be labeled according to the sex of the person whose salaries are being plotted. The REGRESSION format for the plot causes regression statistics to be printed below the plot. See Figure 9. The regression statistics are computed for all cases taken together. To obtain separate plots and separate statistics for males and females, you could use SPSS-X or SPSS/PC+ utilities to select cases; or you could use the more sophisticated REGRESSION procedure, which offers many facilities for testing subgroups and residuals.

Sample job

Figure 2   Map of variables on the active file following
            update

```
MAP OF THE RESULT FILE

RESULT      EMPDATA1   *     RESULT      EMPDATA1   *
------      --------   -     ------      ----------  -
ID          ID         ID    EDLEVEL     EDLEVEL
SALBEG      SALBEG           WORK        WORK
SEX         SEX              JOBCAT      JOBCAT
TIME        TIME             MINORITY    MINORITY
AGE         AGE              SEXRACE     SEXRACE
SALNOW      SALNOW     SALNOW  BEGDATE   BEGDATE
```

Figure 3   Output from LIST

```
   ID      BEGDATE       SALNOW      AVGRAISE

  626    13-JUN-1984     10680     $1,760.00
  632    17-JUL-1983     21960     $2,940.00
  637    14-MAR-1985     27250     $7,127.00
  642    17-JUL-1982     10620     $   984.00
  652    20-MAR-1961     12300     $   320.77
  658    17-AUG-1975     22800     $1,000.00
  664    15-FEB-1980      8040     $   394.00
  671    13-SEP-1980     10380     $   580.00
  679    19-SEP-1956      9000     $   100.00
  688    16-MAY-1981      9600     $   860.00

NUMBER OF CASES READ  =  50  NUMBER OF CASES LISTED = 10
```

Figure 4   Output from FREQUENCIES for SALNOW

SALNOW   CURRENT SALARY

      COUNT   MIDPOINT   ONE SYMBOL EQUALS APPROXIMATELY 4.00
                             OCCURRENCES

         39   7430   **********
        101   9702   ************************
        102   11974   *************************
         41   14246   **********
         22   16518   ******
         13   18790   ***
         14   21062   ****
         11   23334   ***
          9   25606   **
          9   27878   **
          4   30150   *
          5   32422   *
          1   34694
          3   36966   *
          2   39238   *
          2   41510   *
          1   43782
          0   46054
          0   48326
          0   50598
          1   52870

          I....+....I....+....I....+....I....+....I....+....I
          0   40   80   120   160   200
                          HISTOGRAM FREQUENCY

MEAN   14173.297 STD DEV 7052.698   MINIMUM   6300.000
MAXIMUM   54000.000

VALID CASES   380   MISSING CASES 0

FIGURE 5   Output from FREQUENCIES for MINORITY

MINORITY   MINORITY CLASSIFICATION

VALUE LABEL	VALUE	FREQUENCY	PERCENT	VALID PERCENT	CUM PERCENT
WHITE	0	288	75.8	75.8	75.8
NONWHITE	1	92	24.2	24.2	100.0
	TOTAL	380	100.0	100.0	

```
            I
        0   ----------------------------------------+
   WHITE    I                                    288 I
            ----------------------------------------+
            I
        1   ------------+
NONWHITE    I      92 I
            ------------+
            I
            I.........I.........I.........I.........I.........I
            0        80       160       240       320       400
                              FREQUENCY
```

MEAN   .232   STD DEV   .429   MINIMUM   .000
MAXIMUM 1.000

VALID CASES   380   MISSING CASES   0

Figure 6   Crosstabulation of MINORITY and SEX

- - - - - - - C R O S S T A B U L A T I O N   OF - - - - - - - -

    MINORITY   MINORITY CLASSIFICATION
  BY SEX   SEX OF EMPLOYEE
- -PAGE 1 OF 1

		SEX MALES	FEMALES	COUNT ROW TOTAL
		0	1	
MINORITY				
WHITE	0	181	107	288 75.8
NONWHITE	1	61	31	92 24.2
COLUMN TOTAL		242 63.7	138 36.3	380 100.0

CHI-SQUARE	D.F.	SIGNIFICANCE	MIN E.F.	CELLS WITH E.F.< 5
0.22635	1	0.6342	33.411	NONE
0.36033	1	0.5483	(BEFORE YATES CORRECTION)	

NUMBER OF MISSING OBSERVATIONS = 0

Sample job

Figure 7   'MEANS
            output:
            average
            salary
            increase
            by minority
            and
            sex

D E S C R I P T I O N   O F   S U B P O P U L A T I O N S

Criterion Variable   AVGRAISE   AVERAGE ANNUAL RAISE
    Broken Down by   MINORITY   MINORITY CLASSIFICATION
                by   SEX   SEX OF EMPLOYEE

Variable	Value	Label	Mean	Std Dev	Cases
For Entire Population			2221.0198	3322.6981	380
MINORITY	0	WHITE	2622.1633	3692.1118	288
SEX	0	MALES	2960.2626	4107.9951	181
SEX	1	FEMALES	2050.2382	2779.6308	107
MINORITY	1	NONWHITE	965.2664	940.9329	92
SEX	0	MALES	1054.7018	978.8123	61
SEX	1	FEMALES	789.2804	849.2122	31

Total Cases =   380

Figure 8   'ANOVA
            output:
            effects
            of
            minority
            and
            sex
            on
            salary
            increase

---

* * * A N A L Y S I S   O F   V A R I A N C E * * *

	AVGRAISE	AVERAGE ANNUAL RAISE
by	MINORITY	MINORITY CLASSIFICATION
	SEX	SEX OF EMPLOYEE

Source of Variation	Sum of Squares	DF	Mean Square	F	Sig of F
Main Effects	242016797	2	121008398.737	11.561	.000
MINORITY	197344741	1	197344740.998	18.853	.000
SEX	50596626	1	50596626.420	4.834	.029
2-Way Interactions	6541229	1	6541228.505	.625	.430
MINORITY SEX	6541229	1	6541228.505	.625	.430
Explained	248558026	3	82852675.326	7.915	.000
Residual	3935724290	376	10467351.835		
Total	4184282316	379	11040322.734		

380 cases were processed.
0 cases (.0 pct) were missing.

Figure 9   PLOT output: current salary by beginning salary

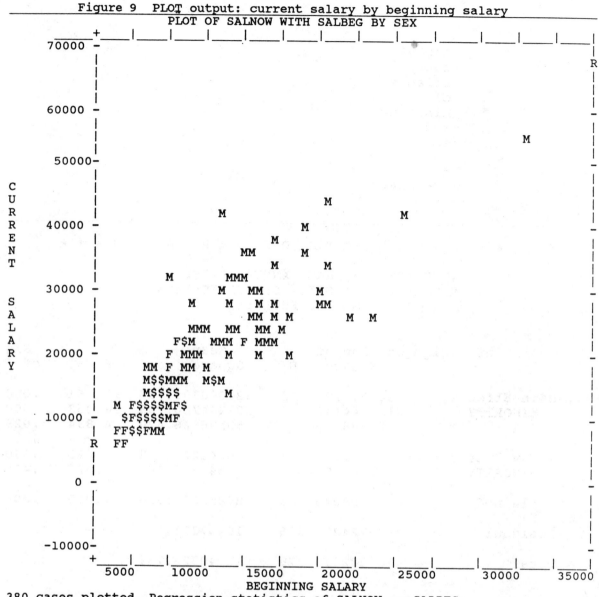

380 cases plotted. Regression statistics of SALNOW on SALBEG;
Correlation .88135 R squared .77677   S.E. of Est 3336.58334 Sig. .0000
Intercept(S.E.) 756.05799(407.62695) Slope(S.E.) 1.887301 (.05204)
M:MALES   F:FEMALES $:MULTIPLES OCCURENCE